The Practitioner Inquiry Series

Marilyn Cochran-Smith and Susan L. Lytle, *SERIES EDITORS*

(continued)

Re-Reading Families

The Literate Lives of Urban Children, Four Years Later

CATHERINE COMPTON-LILLY

FOREWORD BY JAMES PAUL GEE

Teachers College, Columbia University
New York and London

Published by Teachers College Press, 1234 Amsterdam Avenue, New York, NY 10027
Copyright © 2007 by Teachers College, Columbia University

Portions of Chapters 1 and 2 appeared previously in the following articles:
Compton-Lilly, C. (2005). "Sounding Out": A pervasive model of reading. *Language Arts* *82*(6), 441–451. Copyright 2005 by the National Council of Teachers of English. Reprinted with permission.
Novinger, S. & Compton-Lilly, C. (2005). Telling our stories: Speaking truth to power. *Language Arts 82*(3), 195–203. Copyright 2005 by the National Council of Teachers of English. Reprinted with permission.

Library of Congress Cataloging-in-Publication Data

Compton-Lilly, Catherine.
  Re-reading families : the literate lives of urban children, four years later /
Catherine Compton-Lilly ; foreword by James Paul Gee.
    p. cm. — (The practitioner inquiry series)
  Follow-up to author's earlier work, Reading families. New York : Teachers College Press, c2003.
  InAuthorudes bibliographical references and index.
  Follow-up to author's earlier work, Reading families. New York : Teachers College Press, c2003.
  ISBN 13: 978-0-8077-4792-6 (hardcover)
  ISBN 10: 0-8077-4792-0 (hardcover)
  ISBN 13: 978-0-8077-4791-9 (pbk.)
  ISBN 10: 0-8077-4791-2 (pbk.)
  1. City children—Education—United States—Case studies. 2. City children—Books and reading—United States—Case studies. 3. Reading—Parent participation—United States—Case studies. 4. Education, Urban—United States—Case studies. I. Title.
  LC5131.C617 2007
  372.42'5—dc22

                                                                                    2007000217

ISBN: 978-0-8077-4791-9 (paper)
ISBN: 978-0-8077-4792-6 (hardcover)

Printed on acid-free paper
Manufactured in the United States of America

14   13   12   11   10   09   08   07   8   7   6   5   4   3   2   1

As always, I dedicate this book to Todd and Carly.

Thanks for being with me.

Contents

Foreword

In his 1986 book, *The Real Coke, the Real Story*, Thomas Oliver tells the story of the now infamous "New Coke," a story retold in Malcolm Gladwell's (2005) best-seller *Blink*. In the early 1980s, Pepsi ran commercials in which people took a sip from two glasses, not knowing which was Coke and which Pepsi. The majority said they preferred Pepsi. The Coca-Cola Company replicated the tests and found, to their chagrin, the same result. Afraid of losing market share, Coke—long the dominant brand—changed its old formula and came out with the New Coke, which was made to a new formula, one that in a new round of blind taste tests came out above Pepsi. But New Coke was a disaster. Consumers hated it. Coke returned to its old formula, and Pepsi never did overtake Coke. What happened here? What was wrong with the test?

In a sip test, tasters don't drink an entire bottle or can of soda—they just take a sip. It turns out that if you ask people not just to take a sip, but to take a case or two of each drink home for a few weeks, you often get a different result. Taking a sip of a drink and drinking a whole bottle or can are different experiences. Sometimes, for example, the first sip is sweet, but the whole bottle is, by the end, cloying. Furthermore, people report their taste preferences differently when they are drinking at home than they do when they are drinking in a lab under artificial conditions.

There is nothing "unscientific" about a sip taste—it's a nice controlled sort of study of a rather classic sort. But it is misleading and in the case of New Coke, disastrously so. To truly know people's preferences you need to know how the product is situated in and placed within the lived social practices of the person and his or her interpretations of those practices. A sociocultural-situated view of language, learning, and the mind takes the same view of people's talents. To fairly and truly judge what a person can do you need to know how the talent (i.e., skill, knowledge) you are assessing is situated in, placed within, the lived social practices of the person and his or her interpretations of those practices. Like sip tests, many a standardized test can be perfectly "scientific" and useless at the same time; worse, it, too, can be disastrous.

Catherine Compton-Lilly's brilliant book *Rereading Families* is here to tell you exactly why the reading tests we use in school are often no better than Pepsi's sip test. She will show you, loudly and clearly, what it really means to investigate children's reading. If we heed her words, we will not continue to give our children the equivalent of New Coke in our literacy classrooms.

—*James Paul Gee*

REFERENCES

Gladwell, M. (2005). *Blink.* New York: Little, Brown.
Oliver, T. (1986). *The real coke, the real story.* New York: Random House.

Acknowledgments

Writing is truly a social practice and many people have been involved in the conception and the writing of this book. I have been fortunate to be surrounded by friends and colleagues who inspired me and supported me through both the research and the writing processes.

I would like to first thank the families who welcomed me back for the second phase of the research. Their thoughts and insights have truly transformed me. I am extremely grateful for their generosity and their willingness to allow me to share their words with others. I am constantly in awe of their strength and the commitment they make to their children.

Teacher research grants from the National Council of Teachers of English and the International Reading Association funded this phase of the research project, and I am grateful to both these organizations for their continuing support of my work. I would also like to thank the editorial staff at Teachers College Press, and in particular Carol Collins and Lori Tate for their unending faith.

Finally, I continuously thank my family, Todd and Carly, for helping me to follow my dreams and joining me on the journey.

Four Years Later: The Role of Reading in Students' Lives

Alicia, Grade 1

Author: What's your favorite book?

Alicia: School books.

Author: Which ones at school?

Alicia: It's about the Itsy Bitsy Spider.

Author: Mmm-hmm, what else?

Alicia: (pause) Uh, the one gorilla [book].

Author: Mmm-hmm. Anything else?

Alicia: That's all.

Alicia, Grade 5

Author: What kind of things do you read?

Alicia: I read chapter books and I read baby books and sometimes I read to my sister. And I read big, big dictionaries. And that's it.

Author: What's your favorite thing to read?

Alicia: Chapter books.

Author: Like, which ones?

Alicia: Babysitters Club.

Author: Have you read them all yet?

Alicia: No.

Author: No. How many have you read?

Alicia: I read like eight of them.

Our students are not stagnant. They are continuously growing and learning at home, in school, and in their communities. As teachers and researchers, we meet children at particular times in their lives. I met Alicia when she was in my first-grade class at Rosa Parks School; she reported enjoying the storybooks that we read at school; 4 years later she was reading books from the *Babysitters Club* series (Martin & Lerangis, 1986–2000).

Marvin, Grade 1	Marvin, Grade 5

Marvin: I read (pause) newspaper.
Author: Mmm-hmm, what else?
Marvin: I read notebooks.
Author: Mmm-hmm.
Marvin: I read library books.
Author: Good, what else?
Marvin: I read math.
Author: Mmm-hmmm.
Marvin: I read mail.
	Author: What kind of things do
	    you like to read?
	Marvin: Goosebumps.
	Author: Yeah. You take after your
	    Grandpa here. Anything else?
	Marvin: Nate The Great.
	Author: What else? There's
	    mystery and horror for you
	    right there.
	Mr. Sherwood: He likes Pokemon.

In first grade, Marvin listed general genres of text but did not name any titles; in fifth grade, like Alicia, he mentions popular book series. How are these children's reading practices and preferences related to home, school, and the people who inhabit these contexts? Does Alicia's interest in the *Babysitter's Club* reflect her mother's love of novels? Or are her friends at school or in the neighborhood reading books from the series? Is Marvin's interest in horror and mystery related to his grandfather's interests in these same topics or to the other boys his age who also tell me they love *Goosebumps* books (Stine, 1992–1997)? What is changing for these children as readers and how are these changes embedded in their lives?

Changing tastes and interests in books are expected as children move through school, but what other changes occur in reference to reading and how are those changes caught up with children's experiences, families, and peers? In this book, I examine the reading lives of a group of 10 urban students and their families over time. As the children's first-grade teacher, I was deeply committed to helping Alicia, Marvin, and their classmates learn to read. On these pages, I follow the children across time and revisit them in Grades 4 and 5 to understand their reading and school experiences as they progress through elementary school.

As educators and researchers, we work with children for a few months and attempt to make sense of their experiences. A few months or perhaps a school year are often the parameters of our teaching and researching efforts. This book is about what we learn when we expand those parameters and follow students and their families over time as they move through elementary school. We often fail to recognize that children experience, like all of us, their worlds across time and that those experiences have effects that accumulate over time. For both of the young readers presented above and their classmates, reading development, reading ability, peer interests, teacher influences, family role models, literacy practices at home and school, and the experiences of siblings all contribute to who they are as readers at various points in their lives.

Our tendency as researchers to focus on short periods of time is related to constraints that accompany the research process, involving time, costs, and access that often limit our studies. Our efforts are snapshots, short time-bound glimpses into schools and students' lives. Due to the organization of schools, we tend to focus on students and teachers in one class, during one school year but we often forget to ask what happens as children move through school. How do their experiences and the experiences of their family members and friends cumulate to construct understandings about reading, schooling, and the world? Students exist within families, schools, and communities that bring particular understandings about the world. Students, parents, and teachers inhabit spaces that are complex and changing. Families move, children change schools, children are tested for special education, brothers and sisters go to college or drop out of high school, family finances change, and family members are born and die.

A fourth-grade special education student was not always a special education student and the well-behaved student may not have always assumed that role. In first grade, Ms. Hudson described her son, Jermaine, as being "stubborn"; by fourth grade he had been retained once and was classified as having a learning disability

Jermaine, Grade 1

Author: Ok, what's it been like helping Jermaine to read?

Ms. Hudson: Mmm. He's stubborn at times.

Author: He sure is. Why do you think he's so stubborn?

Ms. Hudson: Because he think he's missing something outside. He wants to be outside and play.

Jermaine Grade 4

Ms. Hudson: His reading is still below level. They had a meeting at the Board of Education for him to get like a tutor 3 days out of the week. What days is it?

Jermaine: Monday, Tuesday, and Wednesday.

Ms. Hudson: Right. Monday, Tuesday, and Wednesday and they got them down as I think it's [a] learning disability. They [the Board of Education] don't want to give him no help like that, but me and his teacher talked them into it.

What was once defined as stubbornness is now labeled as disability.

Javon was also a challenging student in first grade. Although he had few difficulties academically, his behavior could be difficult for both his teacher and his mother. By fifth grade, Ms. Mason reports that Javon was cooperating well with his teachers in school.

Javon, Grade 1	Javon, Grade 5
Ms. Mason: His attitude. If I can get him settled down long enough and with a story that he want to know about, I don't have any problem. But Javon, he loves to play a lot. So I have to find something that he really loves to do.	*Ms. Mason:* He [Javon] say, "I want my teacher to like me." And I talked to him. I told him. I said, "If you change your personality and stop acting out," and I said, "your teacher will like you." *Author:* That's for sure. *Ms. Mason:* He was so proud. Yeah. *Author:* Sounds like he had a good year last year. *Ms. Mason:* Oh he did. Because him and I had a talk before he even started, that he was saying about he wanted his teacher to like him. He's tired, he ain't getting in trouble all the time. I told him. I'd say, "You've got to change your personality." Sometimes you overlook—sometimes a person might say something you don't like, but you have to overlook it sometimes.

In schools, agency and activity coexist alongside various situations and opportunities. There are good and bad school experiences that affect the trajectories of children. There are changes in families that can positively or negatively affect children at school. Time and change are constant, yet we often treat children and families as stagnant entities. We must remember that urban families are not static sets of pathologies that hold children back. They are active communities that work to access resources to support their children. Experiences accumulate for students but also accumulate within families. Families learn about how schools operate.

Parents actively work within the systems that are offered to obtain the best educational experiences they can for their children. Ms. Rodriguez notes that many children slip through school without learning what they need. She explains that parents play a role in preventing this from happening.

Ms. Rodriguez: See, I come from New York. So, with us it's—in New York a lot of times you slip through that system and you just skid. The kids get pushed through school without learning anything. And I refuse to let that happen to mine. I refuse it! And it got to the point where even when we got up here, it's, you have to be that parent that actually cares and let them know that you care and let them know you're not going to, they're not going to push your child through school when they don't know anything.
Author: So, do you—what do you have to do to let them know that? What kind of things do you have to do?
Ms. Rodriguez: Um, write letters, show up at school meetings and talk to the teachers.

DEMOGRAPHICS AND ACHIEVEMENT

What are the options and choices for children as they move through school? The statistics tell us that reading achievement in urban schools is below state and national averages. For example, in 2003 only 14% of major urban school districts had half or more of their students obtain reading scores commensurate with or above their state's average (Council of the Great City Schools, 2004). In 1998 the graduation rate was 22% lower for African American students and 24% lower for Latino students than their White counterparts. Only 56% of African American students and 54% of Latino students graduated from high school (Manhattan Institute for Policy Research, 2001). Furthermore in the year 2000 only 17% of African American students earned at least a bachelor's degree as compared to 28% of demographically comparable European American students.

Whenever I confront statistics such as these I am left wondering: "Will these statistics prove true for my students?" In part, this book is an attempt to answer this question, but even more it is a quest to reveal what these statistics do not tell us. What are the experiences and situations that my students encounter as they move through school? How do they interact with school and the educational experiences we have provided for them? And finally, what role does reading play in their school experiences?

When I returned to speak with my former first-grade students and their parents, the students were in fourth or fifth grade. Some were doing well in school, some had been retained, and others had been placed in special education classes. Family experiences also varied. Some siblings had dropped out of school; others had jobs or were in college. Some previously unemployed parents were now working; others were on disability; and still others were working at the same jobs they held when their children were my students. A parent had died; a sister was born; children had been placed in a foster home; an older sister had run away; a brother was arrested; a cousin was shot; siblings had graduated from high school; and an older brother had a college scholarship.

Having helped my former students learn to read, I wanted to know them now as readers. What role did reading play in their fourth- and fifth-grade lives? What books were they reading and what were their attitudes toward reading? What were their feelings about school and how had they experienced the educational opportunities that had been provided? I also wanted to understand the ways parents made sense of the educational experiences of their children. How were parents experiencing the school experiences of their children and the accompanying literacy expectations? What were their challenges and what resources did they bring?

When I visited my former students, I could see the faces and the smiles of the 6-year-olds, yet I was thrilled to meet the young people they had become. Generally the children were still excited to see me and they all participated in all aspects of the interviews. Their parents seemed to have clearer recollections of me and their children's experiences in first grade than the children did. Parents asked about my family and wanted to know where I was working. Most of the children had few memories of first grade and they often asked me confirm fleeting memories of what they thought they remembered.

With regard to their reading progress, most of the children were reading within a year of their grade level as measured by running records of leveled texts (see Table I.1). The three exceptions are Jermaine and Bradford, who have both been provided with special education services, and Peter, who was reading above grade level. What this figure does not show is that many of the children had significant difficulties retelling or answering questions about the texts they read. When asked about reading, few of the children mentioned books that had been assigned in school. Some mentioned books that were significantly below their reading level while others were interested in popular fiction, especially books by R. L. Stine (1992–1997; 1989–present). Only three of the students passed the fourth-grade ELA test.

Table I.1. Reading Proficiency

	End of Grade 1	End of Grade 4/5	ELA test
Christy	Grade 2	Grade 4	Failed
David	Late Grade 1	Grade 4	Failed
Angela	*	Grade 5	Passed
Jasmine	Grade 2	Grade 4	Failed
Javon	Grade 2	Grade 5	Passed
Bradford	Early Grade 1	Grade 2	Failed
Peter	Grade 2	Grade 7	Passed
Jermaine	Grade 1	Grade 2	Failed
Alicia	Grade 2	Grade 4	Failed
Marvin	Late Grade 1	Grade 4	Failed

* Angela was added to the sample when she was in fifth grade.

THE IMPORTANCE OF LONGITUDINAL QUALITATIVE RESEARCH

This book, as well as its predecessor, *Reading Families* (Compton-Lilly, 2003), evolved out of 18 years of teaching primary-grade students in both urban and suburban schools and my concerns about the difficulties children faced when learning to read. Although my students are generally intelligent and capable, mastering reading was often challenging. Based on my own research and the research of others (Bartoli, 1995; Bauman & Thomas, 1997; Fine & Weis, 1998; Nieto, 1996; Taylor & Dorsey-Gaines, 1988), I know that families of urban students are interested and involved in helping their children become good readers. The difficulties that my students faced could not be blamed on families.

The initial phase of my research, which was completed when the student participants were my first-grade students, was intended to be a yearlong doctoral dissertation study. However, after completing that study and writing about the children, I decided to return to the families when the children were in fourth and fifth grade to discover what had happened since first grade. I am still in contact with 8 of the original 10 families, and my intention is to extend the study further.

The following question drove this second phase of my longitudinal research project: *Why do urban students often have difficulty becoming proficient readers?* For this phase, I conducted a series of follow-up interviews with the same children and parents I worked with 4 years earlier (see Appendix A for family information). Interviews focused on the children's experiences with learning to read, self-assessment of their reading abilities, critical events in their lives as readers, and their feelings about reading as they progress through school. In addition to collecting prompted writing samples, I conducted student reading assessments (Beaver, 1997). (See Appendix B for methodological details about my study.)

The longitudinal nature of this project is important. Very few researchers have had the opportunity to follow small groups of children for significant amounts of time. I argue that longitudinal qualitative research is critical if we are to understand the schooling experiences of children. As I reflect on the children in this study, I am reminded of the vast stores of information I have collected. I know that David's progress in learning to read started out slowly in first grade but he later caught up and did well. I know that Peter was always one of the best readers in the class and that Jermaine struggled with reading and writing even after I spent 20 weeks working with him one-on-one as his Reading Recovery teacher.

Traditionally qualitative research has sought to capture "thick description" (Geertz, 1973) of people's experiences and to make sense of the local worlds that people inhabit. This goal challenges researchers to document their "interpretations of [the] interpretations" that people make about their worlds. I suggest that there is a thickness or depth relative to time that is tapped by examining local phenomena and people's interpretation of local phenomena over time. Depth across time has the potential to reveal the cumulative effects of experiences on people's lives including experiences associated with schooling.

Longitudinal qualitative research has particular relevance to the study of disenfranchised populations. Longitudinal studies have the potential to reveal the cumulative effects of racism, classism, and sexism by following individual students and groups of students across time and revealing the processes that contribute to the long-term effects of attending underfunded schooling, participating in racist/classist/sexist educational practices, experiencing well-intended but discriminative practices of educators, and witnessing negative assumptions held by educators about various groups of students. Racism, classism, and sexism are not about one teacher and one class. Experiences of racism, classism, and sexism start long before children enter school and continue after they leave school; they are experienced across generations and shared among family members and friends. Longitudinal research has the potential to reveal how these experiences accumulate over time and how children make sense of those experiences.

RACE AND RESEARCH

As educators and researchers, we must constantly guard against what Enciso (2003) refers to as "deceptions of self." She describes these as moments in which we think we know and understand the world around us. Enciso warns that knowing closes down the possibility of disrupting accepted ways of understanding the world. She encourages us to seek "strategic spaces that expose and possibly interrupt the construction of hierarchies of status, difference, and meaning" (p. 173). In my research, race is a salient issue that I have only erratically examined.

When I reflect on the data presented in *Reading Families* (Compton-Lilly, 2003), I am struck by the silences that surround race. I was a White teacher speaking with Puerto Rican and African American parents and children about reading and their school experiences, yet race was rarely mentioned in the interviews nor explored in my writing. During the interviews, we discussed many sensitive areas including welfare, parents' own school experiences, parents' hopes for their children, health issues, legal matters, employment, money, social services, politics, and even religion; but not race.

During the second phase of my research, I made the decision to speak directly about race. I waited until the second round of interviews to raise the topic because I was genuinely fearful that parents would be offended. By asking about race would I be suggesting that race matters? If the parents had not raised the issue of race, was it appropriate for me to raise the issue? Perhaps they avoided the topic for a reason.

When I look back at my data, I am struck by how cautiously and indirectly I couched my questions. I asked each of the parents of my students slight variations of the following questions:

- Do you think that schools discriminate against certain groups of people?
- Do you think that schools help some groups of children more than others?

Notably, my questions never mention race. I adopted safer words that referenced "groups of people." The only word that pointed to race was the word "discriminate"; I remember giving careful thought to how I worded this question. Luckily the parents understood my intent and responded in terms of race.

Six of the nine parents whom I asked reported that schools did not discriminate against particular groups of students; the others disagreed. Interestingly the three parents who identified schools as racist are all families with children who were attending middle and high schools. Although older children were often nearby during interviews, these data samples are among the few occasions when older children participated. They would chime in from an adjoining room or suspend their television viewing to participate.

There is no simple answer as to whether race matters in urban schools. For the families who believed that race plays a role in schooling, several did not accept race as a formidable obstacle. Parents know the rules of the game of school and are willing to play. The question remains whether parental caring and adopting expected norms is enough to counteract racism when schools are structured in racist ways (Villenas & Deyhle, 1999).

THE PURPOSES OF THIS BOOK

This book has been crafted with two primary intentions:

1. To explore the reading experiences of a group of children and their parents over time within a complex field that involves particular personal, family, and cultural histories; current situations and experiences; and hopes and expectations for the future. I explore reading over time by looking across a small sample of students and their parents to identify themes and patterns and by constructing paired case studies of students.
2. To share one model of longitudinal ethnographic research and explore the potential of this type of research to help educators understand the experiences of students as they progress through school. If race, poverty, and difference are explanations for the officially defined failure of large numbers of children from diverse backgrounds, it is very possible that this failure is the result of cumulating experiences. This research begins to illustrate how various experiences converge over time resulting in positionings and ways of being that make school success either inevitable or difficult to obtain.

Grand narratives that surround urban children and urban schooling tell us that parents don't care and that violent neighborhoods will produce violent youth. These stories about families and communities are voiced alongside stories of negligent and uncaring teachers. In the midst of educational reports, test score statistics, and research papers, accounts of what actually happens to children as they pass through school are extremely rare.

This book is my attempt to complicate and challenge the grand narratives by presenting stories grounded in the experiences of children and their families over multiple years of schooling. Specifically, I am interested in issues related to reading that arise for children and parents as children progress through school: What challenges do families face and how do they deal with these challenges? And what are the hopes and dreams of children and parents that are not reflected in grand narratives that blame families, communities, and teachers? What is the long-term role of reading in the school experiences of children?

As in *Reading Families* (Compton-Lilly, 2003), listening to the voices of children and parents has greatly informed my teaching and my thinking. It has revealed different ways of understanding the world. I hear the commonly accepted ways of understanding the world: "Urban parents don't care," "I read by sounding out words," "Testing kids will ensure that kids learn." But I witnessed conflicting information: I learned that most parents in urban communities care greatly about heir children, children rarely sound out words when they read, and parents describe the damage caused to their children by high-stakes testing. This book begins to name and examine assumptions about reading and urban families while revealing alternate understandings. Sometimes people directly challenge widely held assumptions about the world. At other times their actions, experiences, or the situation challenge these unquestioned assumptions.

Assumptions about the world do not operate only at particular times; they operate over long periods of time acting on people and families within the context of lived experiences. These understandings never stagnate. What children believed and hoped in first grade may not be the same as what they believe and hope in fifth grade, and parental beliefs may change as well. Maintaining faith in assumptions about the world can require ignoring or downplaying one's own experiences. It may require people to separate their beliefs from their experiences. The inability of simplistic explanations to account for lived experiences can become problematic. Slogans that promote "working hard in school," "staying in school," and "getting a diploma" ring hollow over time. I suspect that it is more than coincidence that the strongest critique of schools and teachers voiced in this study comes from families with older children who are in high school and beyond. Their children's school experiences have demonstrated the inadequacy of simple slogans.

THE PLAN OF THIS BOOK

Chapter 1 of this book presents a theoretical framework that grounds the current phase of the study. Specifically, I present information about dominant and alternative discourses as well as explore the role discourses play in reading and literacy instruction. In addition, I present the concept of "figured worlds" (Holland, Lachiotte, Skinner, & Cain, 1998) to examine how discourses act upon people while people simultaneously act upon their worlds; the concept of figured worlds links dominant and alternative discourses with identity formation and agency.

In Chapter 2, I present two dominant discourses that operate within the figured worlds of parents and children. Specifically, I explore the importance of paying attention in school and the ways parents and children talk about high-stakes testing. To account for the difficulties some children have in school, parents and children speak extensively about the importance of paying attention and identify the lack of attention as the source of school difficulties. I challenge this dominant discourse by exploring conceptions of attention and suggesting that simplistic formulas that equate attention with learning are inadequate. While parents describe the potential of high-stakes tests to lead to educational equity for their children, they simultaneously tell stories that reveal the violence high-stakes testing wreaks on children's lives

In the remaining chapters, I present rich case studies to illustrate themes from my research. Chapter 3 explores complexities related to the identity development of two boys. Chapter 4 explores identity construction in the cases of two girls. In Chapter 5, the school success of two students is explored in terms of the types of "reading capital" students display and how those ways of being and knowing are valued in classrooms.

The book closes with a chapter that brings together many of the ideas presented in earlier chapters and provides the reader with general recommendations both for teaching in diverse communities and for conducting longitudinal research in these same communities. Finally, the appendices offer the reader a general overview of the children and their families and details about my research methodology.

Chapter 1

Discourses and Figured Worlds

When I asked my former first-grade students how things were going in fourth and fifth grades, they offered a range of responses:

Marvin: I stay out of the office.
Alicia: Some of my classes get on my nerves like usual.
Jermaine: The reason at my school that I don't like nobody [is] because they like to start shoving me.
Javon: I met a lot of friends.

As the children's former teacher and as a researcher who has worked closely with these families in the past, I read each of the children's comments alongside my prior knowledge of the children. I knew that Marvin spent a lot of time in the principal's office in the past. Alicia was generally a cooperative and enthusiastic student. Jermaine always struggled to make friends and to fit in with the other boys, and Javon was very popular with the other children. The fourth- and fifth-grade years are a chapter in the children's lives. Yet this chapter, like their prior experiences, occurs within a particular local context that includes neighborhoods, schools, and a particular school district. Each child is involved in a unique journey, yet all share a local context, the same context in which I taught for 16 years.

FOCUSING ON THE CONTEXT

Two years after the data for this book were collected, a letter to the editor appeared in the local paper entitled "Growing up in the 50s." The writer reminisced about the neighborhood that surrounds Rosa Parks School:

We had Ralph's Sweet Shop on the corner where all the kids hung out. It was next door to the Lyric Theater; it cost 35 cents to see a movie. With a dollar we could go to a movie, have popcorn and pop

13

and go next door for Cokes, hotdogs and jukebox music. There was
also a soda shop and we went there too. What a great time to grow
up! No guns, drugs, or garbage. A time when kids obeyed their parents and had to be home before the street lights went on. . . It's a
shame that the parents of today let their children grow up too fast.
Consider the style of clothes the kids wear and the makeup and
all. Parents, unite and take over the home again. Learn to say no;
it won't kill your children, but saying yes all the time may. It was a
wonderful time in the fifties.

The writer of this editorial revisits a past time; the description is nostal-
gic. Years ago, children in the community that surrounded my school
went to the movies and hung out at the sweet shop drinking Cokes and
listening to music. They wore the right clothes, obeyed their parents, and
were home at dusk. The author compares these children of the past with
the children of today who "grow up too fast" because their parents let
them. Yet, when placed in its historical context another story needs to be
told; this story forces us to ask whose experiences are described in this
idyllic scenario and whose are not.

On July 25, 1964, riots broke out in the same neighborhood and only
ended 3 days later after intervention from the National Guard. Five people
had died, 350 were injured, and more than 900 people were arrested. Community leaders attributed the riots to the anger of African American residents who were frustrated by unequal opportunities for jobs, education,
and housing as well as tense relations with law enforcement agencies.
During the 3 years that had led up to the riots numerous instances of
police brutality and abuse had been reported in the local press (Rayam &
Memmott, 2004).

The editorial's idyllic story of sweet shops and movie theaters tells
nothing of the inequity and the injustice that characterized life for the
city's African American residents during the 1950s. It does not mention
the substandard housing and the dearth of employment opportunities
that were available to African American families.

The housing projects that currently surround Rosa Parks School and
the school itself were built in the years following the riots as part of various initiatives designed to address racial injustice. Children were bused
from this neighborhood to attend schools that bordered the growing
suburbs, and programs were established in local colleges and businesses
to provide opportunities for African American students and employees.
There is a large field in front of the Henry Ford School where I taught at
the time of these interviews. Prior to the riots, houses stood there; they
were damaged and later torn down as part of the urban renewal efforts

that followed the riots. The scars of racial unrest are visible throughout the neighborhood.

Today, the busing program has long been discontinued and the housing projects are over 30 years old. When I began teaching at Rosa Parks School in 1988, I was shocked to discover that fewer than ten White students were among the over 1,000 children enrolled.

The community around Rosa Parks School has changed very little since the riots. A couple of years ago a new supermarket opened across the street from the school adjacent to a small plaza that houses a police substation, an urban clothing store, and a dollar store. A new McDonalds fast-food restaurant sits on the corner. Income levels for people in the school community are almost $10,000 below African American families in other parts of the city and less than half the income of all families in the county (Rayam & Memmott, 2004). Only 6% of African American people in this community have a college degree; this is a small increase over the 2% who held college degrees in 1960 (Hare & Orman, 2004).

In recent years, research focusing on local communities has helped educators to understand the unique dynamics of the communities in which we work. Freebody, Muspratt, and Dwyer (2001) describe a recent interest in highlighting "the distinctiveness of local sites of social activity and the multiplicity of social actions on those sites" (p. vii). This focus on local sites challenges the existence of uniform ways of being literate, uniform definitions of literacy competence, and uniform interpretations of textual meanings, and has revealed the multiple ways reading is understood and used in various communities. The stories of my students and their families reveal their experiences with reading. They live within a particular community, learned to read within a particular classroom, and attend school within a particular school and school district. My work focuses on reading in this local community over time and follows my former students and their families through elementary school as they live and learn at home and at school.

It is critical to understand that the local community my students and their parents inhabit is connected to larger communities and to society; one of these links involves the discourses that are shared between the local context in which I teach and macrocontexts that extend beyond the parameters of my school community. Ways of being, knowing, and thinking about particular issues and groups of people are often accepted and unquestioned as they circulate across communities acting as generally accepted beliefs; these understandings about the world are routinely voiced in my school community and contribute to the ways the children, parents, and teachers in this community view urban students and understand reading.

CONSIDERING DISCOURSES

In *Reading Families* (Compton-Lilly, 2003), I used the concept of discourses to explore the ways teachers, parents, and children construct their understandings of themselves and their worlds. James Paul Gee (1990) uses "Discourse" in the upper case to describe discourses that are generally accepted within a given community or organization:

> A Discourse is a socially accepted association among ways of using language, of thinking, feeling, believing, valuing, and of acting that can be used to identify oneself as a member of a socially meaningful group or social network or to signal (that one is playing) a socially meaningful role. (p. 131)

Gee explains that we utilize various discourses as we encounter people and situations. When we meet a person, we construct a sense of the "sort" of individual we believe that person to be. We make assumptions based on a person's words, deeds, dress, and deportment, and we are surprised when we learn things about a person that do not fit our predictions.

Discourses entail much more than words. For example, when I conducted the research reported in this book, the ways I dressed, spoke, acted, interacted, and thought positioned me as a member of the teaching staff at my elementary school. Today, the ways I dress, speak, act, interact, and think position me as a faculty member at a major university and there are many times when I am aware of the differences between these two ways of being. Both official and unofficial expectations for professors act upon me and will eventually contribute to whether or not I am deemed successful and granted tenure.

Gee (1990) suggests that the discourses that I am confronting at the university, like all discourses, are socially constructed and reflect the relative power that people wield in the larger society. In *Reading Families,* I referred to discourse communities that were populated by people with relative social, economic, and political power as *mainstream discourses.* These mainstream discourses support existing power structures and the institutions that sustain those power structures and promote "pervasive social theories" about the distribution of material goods and beliefs (Gee, 1990, p. 139). Pervasive social theories suggest that the ways things are is both natural and inevitable. In this volume, I refer to these discourses as *dominant discourses* because I believe that the word *dominant* more aptly captures the power dynamics that accompanies these generally accepted and unquestioned ways of knowing.

Dominant Discourses and Urban Families: "It's Because of Their Parents"

Ms. Rodriguez: A lot of people who are on welfare, if you ask them what they do all day, most of the time they got up late and they sat down in front of that TV and watch the stories and talk shows.

Ms. Johnson: I mean they [students] have, that's because [they have] nothing to encourage them.

David's older sister: Yeah, because of their parents.

Ms. Johnson: It is not only the school. It is the parent involvement also. If you're not involved in your children's education, then you can't expect the school to do it by themselves. You have to be involved, [that is] very big.

At first when I heard the parents of my students describing urban parents negatively, I was surprised. Having worked with parents in this community for several years, I had come to recognize the strengths that my students' parents possessed and brought to the schooling of their children. I did not expect the voices of urban parents to sound so much like my colleagues who often complained about their students' families in the staff room. The words of Ms. Mason who works at a local day care, echoed the comments of my colleagues:

A lot of kids learn how to share through school and still you have parents out there and [they] don't know how to do that. But no, I think the school is great for the kids. Without school a lot of kids would be in bad shape. A lot of kids wouldn't even get to know how to read and that because a lot of parents don't really have time for their kids.

As I continued to listen, I began to understand that not only were teachers subject to making assumptions about urban parents but that people within the community were subject to making the same assumptions about others in this community.

It is important to note that the assumptions voiced by these parents were not true for the 10 randomly selected families involved in this study. I did not consider any of the parents to be lazy; most worked or attended school while raising children and living in a community that offered few amenities and they were all interested in their children's educations. As Gee (1999) maintains, our understandings about the world are not just ideas in our heads. Our knowledge of the world and how it operates entails our ability to "coordinate and be coordinated by constellations of expressions, actions, objects, and people" (p. 19). None of us are immune to adhering to dominant discourses even if those discourses portray us negatively; dominant discourses act on all of us.

Over 25 years ago, Gunther Kress and Robert Hodge (1979) explained how our perceptions of the world "become fixed in language, become a kind of second nature. We inevitably impose our classifications on others, and on ourselves" (p. 5). These collective definitions and socially shared visions are captured by language and in turn affect the ongoing development of language and thought. Because they are deeply embedded in our language and thought, they routinely surface in our actions and interactions. Dominant discourses about urban families are often voiced by professionals as well as members of the general public. Consider the following examples:

- The William F. Goodling Even Start Family Literacy Program offers grant opportunities as part of the Elementary and Secondary Education Act (ESEA). It serves low income parents and "offers promise for helping to break the intergenerational cycle of poverty and low literacy in the Nation" (U.S. Department of Education, 2003a, p. 2). Its goals are to make "sustainable changes in a family" while integrating the following "instructional activities":

    (A) Interactive literacy activities between parents and their children
    (B) Training for parents on how to be the primary teacher for their children and full partners in the education of their children
    (C) Parent literacy training that leads to economic self-sufficiency
    (D) An age-appropriate education to prepare children for success in school and life experiences. (U.S. Department of Education, 2003a, p. 2)

- In a recent editorial in my local paper, a retired high school teacher from my school district reported the following:

    Somehow in the last 50 years, our urban areas have lost those values that kept families healthy even in poverty. It is a shame that our cities have turned into crime-ridden neighborhoods from which good people of any color want to escape.
        The answer to poverty is education. But before education can occur, children must come from loving, stable homes where re-

sponsible adults of any race or nationality assume the work of raising healthy, happy, safe children whose minds are free from anxiety to learn the rigorous material expected of them.

In both of these examples, there are clear implications about what urban families do and do not do for their children. In the first example, the instructional activities that Even Start intends to bestow on urban families include training parents to be their children's "primary teacher" and a "full partner" in their children's educations; the implicit assumption is that without Even Start services poor, urban parents are not their children's first teacher nor are they "full partners." It is also assumed that low-income parents do not participate in "interactive literacy activities" nor prepare children for "success in school and life." These omissions are presented as deficiencies that Even Start is designed to correct. The responsibility for fulfilling these roles is placed solely on the family with the assumption that parents do not know how to help their children.

The second example again places responsibility on the family. In fact, the author of this editorial maintains that changes must occur in families before education can be successful. Parents are held responsible for creating "loving, stable homes" despite their "crime-ridden neighborhoods." In fact, families are expected to reform their neighborhoods through the implementation of healthy family values regardless of the societal challenges that accompany poverty and crime.

Researchers have noted how people's propensities to participate in dominant discourses privilege certain people while acting negatively upon others. Jabari Mahiri (2001) explains that African American youth are often constructed as the "cause, effect, and aberrant response to urban decay" (p. 70). He maintains that "their lives, desires, and dreams are quite different from how they have been constructed in the public spaces of politics and the media" (p. 71). Peter Freebody, Tim Forrest, and Stephanie Gunn (2001) challenge existing discourses that characterize poverty. Although theories of intergenerational poverty, deficit parenting, and negative cultural attributes are often associated with poor families, they suggest that these "discourses of poverty not only reflect but shape 'disadvantage'" (p. 144).

Generally accepted and uninterrogated discourses have been adopted by parents in this study—people whose stories challenge the same discourses they voice. The voicing of dominant discourses reveals tensions. If urban parents are negligent and lazy, how can we account for the remarkable parents in this study? These tensions are obscured by dominant, simplistic messages that equate success with individual achievement, claim equal access, and promise that high standards will lead to equity. Negative assumptions about urban parents coexisting alongside simplistic solutions leaves parents with a limited range of alternatives. Many are alternatives that promise much—"Do well in school so you can get a good job"—but ultimately offer little because doing well in school is only one part of the solution and denies other, more elusive, qualities. However, alterative understandings of the world are always present and these alternative ways of being and knowing constantly challenge dominant discourses.

Alternative Discourses and Urban Families: "Everybody Works"

While the voices of parents presented above subscribe to dominant discourses that berate urban parents, the same parents speak differently when they describe people they know in their neighborhoods:

Ms. Johnson: Well, my next-door neighbor over here actually works for Head Start. So you know she's taught me a lot of different things with teaching and everything. And she's a very caring person.

Ms. Mason: My neighbor that lives downstairs from me, when she see my kids doing something wrong or something, she will always speak to them and that's one thing I like about her.

Ms. Rodriguez also contradicts the assumption that urban parents are lazy and unemployed. She explains that on her block, "everybody works"; she views this as an asset:

Mamie works at the cleaners. . . Doris works in State Hospital. Ronnie works in a factory, her husband is a mechanic. I've seen Mamie's husband, I forgot what he do. And then let's see, Doris's mother's retired but all her kids work. (*Ms. Rodriguez is pointing out the front window to different houses in the neighborhood as she speaks*). . . . Then you got people over here, they just moved there so I don't really know them. But...she works (*pointing to another house*). I see her, everyday she's leaving out for work. Yeah (*laughs*). And Doris's husband works at a motel. So everybody works.

While everyone is subject to the influence and logic of dominant discourses, people's lived experiences can suggest alternative readings of the world that often reveal the failure of dominant discourses to account for their experiences and situations. This is the case for the parents in this study as they talk about their urban neighbors.

Alternative discourses have been identified by other researchers working in diverse communities. Valdes (1996) found that in one Mexican American community none of the residents personally knew people from their community who had "made it" through education. Valdes describes true empowerment as helping "parents understand that, opposed to what many school personnel claim, their children's futures and school success are dependent on a complex set of factors for which they, as parents, are not responsible" (p. 194).

Michele Fine (1993) reports an alternative reading of the world based on her work with urban families. She explains that rather than being the cause of the problems faced by urban children, "low-income mothers are holding together the pieces of a society torn apart by a federal government that, over the past decade, has shown disdain for and has severely punished those living in poverty" (Fine, 1993, p. 688).

While people experience alternative understandings of the world, these experiences can be difficult to conceptualize and voice alongside the deafening din of dominant ways of thinking and being. Gloria Ladson-Billings (2000) maintains that challenging official conceptions of reality requires active effort:

> The process of developing a worldview that differs from the dominant worldview requires active intellectual work on the part of the knower, because schools, society, and the structure and production of knowledge are designed to create individuals who internalize the dominant worldview and knowledge production acquisition processes. (p. 258)

Alternative discourses that are grounded in our lives require each of us to rethink assumptions that are powerfully welded to our understandings of the world. Increasing evidence suggests that parenting and literacy practices are culminations of historical processes within families; changes in these practices persist across generations with change taking more than a single generation (Phillips, Brooks-Gunn, Duncan, Klebanov, & Crane, 1998; Zentella, 1997). The existence of differences among groups of people are grounded in social histories that include fear, shame, bias, racism, privilege, and marginalization.

> The extent to which communities differ on some aspects of outlook and behavior depends in part on the extent of each community's social isolation from the broader society, the material assets or other resources that members of the community control, the privileges and benefits they derive from these resources, the cultural experiences community members have accumulated from political and economic arrangements, both current and historical, and the influence community members wield because of these arrangements. (Wilson, 1998, p. 509)

Thus while the sociohistorical experiences of families and communities have resulted in limited access to resources both past and present, families are blamed when their children arrive at school without access to particular ways of demonstrating literacy competence (i.e., participating in storybook reading, knowing the letters of the alphabet). Histories are ignored and the existence of alternative ways of knowing and being are denied; parents are blamed. Historically constructed discourses of blame do not tell the full story; other ways of understanding the world exist.

The stories of parents in this study reveal alternative readings of their worlds. They describe their own commitment to their children's schooling, their interest in continuing their own educations, and their struggles to stay off welfare and obtain viable employment. They describe their neighbors as people they depend upon and as individuals who are also working hard to hold jobs and raise their children. These stories are powerful challenges to the dominant discourses about families in urban communities.

Dominant Discourses and Reading: "Sound it Out"

Dominant discourses also surround reading. When my students were in first grade, I asked them about solving unknown words and becoming better readers. Almost all of them mentioned "sounding out":

Tiffany: By sounding the letter[s] out.
Christy: Sound it out.
Peter: I sound it out.
Marvin: Sound out the words.

Four years later, I interviewed 9 of these 10 students about reading. They were still talking about "sounding out":

Tiffany: I think they [good readers in the class] sound it out.
Jermaine: They [teachers] make me sound the words out.
Alicia: Like, I need help with a word and she [my mother] be like, "Sound it out."
Marvin: She [the teacher] help me sound out the words.

My students' pervasive use of "sounding out" to describe the reading process fascinated me and my intrigue with "sounding out words" increased when I noted that the parents of my students also spoke extensively about sounding out words. I argue that sounding out is a dominant discourse that pervades the teaching of reading but does not describe what

Figure 1.1. Strategies Available for Solving Unknown Words

First letter: The child appears to have either based his/her attempt on the first letter of the target word or vocalized the first letter, consonant digraph, or consonant blend for a word and then attempted the word (i.e., "/w/ windows" for "windows"; "my" for "mom").

Meaning: The child's attempt reflected attention to the meaning of the story, which may include the text's illustrations (i.e., "sleeping" for "resting").

Syntax miscue: The child produced the wrong form of the correct word (i.e., "ate" for "eat"; "helps" for "help").

Visual similarity: The child's attempts show strong visual similarity to the target word that extends beyond the initial letter; no apparent attempt is made to sound through the word (i.e., "big" for "bag").

Asking: The child asked for help in solving an unknown word.

Sounding out sequential letters: The child used the letters and their sounds in his/her attempts to read sequentially through the word from beginning to ending ("/w/-/a/-/roo/-/m/" for "warm").

Sounding out word parts: The child used letter patterns and/or word parts to attempt a word ("cave-erns" for "caverns").

---

children actually do when reading. While neither children nor parents verbally challenge the importance of sounding out words, analysis of children's actual reading behaviors at Grades 1 and 4/5 reveal that the children in this study very rarely sound out words. Gee's (1990) concept of Discourse applies not just to spoken words but to ways of being and acting. The dominant Discourse is not challenged in words by parents or children, but rather by observation of children's actions in connected texts. Figure 1.1 describes the way I coded children's reading behaviors. Table 1.1 presents the strategies that children used to solve unknown words at Grade 1 and Grades 4 and 5.

Frank Smith (2003) describes "Just Sound Out" as a "Just So Story" that is widely accepted by "newspaper columnists, politicians, and publishers of educational tests and instructional materials" (p. 256). According to Smith, one reason for the prevalence of this belief is that "sounding out can be reduced to small steps, prepackaged in instructional materials, dealt out one bit at a time, and tested and monitored every step of the way" (p. 258). He explains that this belief in sounding out words ". . .can only be undermined by deep and critical thought, which is not evident in

Table 1.1. Strategies Used to Solve Unknown Words

Strategies Used	First Grade		Fourth/Fifth Grade	
	Number of Miscues	Percentage	Number of Miscues	Percentage
First letter	35	59	20	17
Meaning	49	22	21	18
Syntax miscue	14	6	13	11
Visual similarity	21	9	58	50
Asking	4	2	0	0
Sounding out sequential letters	2	1	0	0
Sounding out word parts	3	1	4	4
Totals	228	100	116	100

most casual conversations, media discussions, political pronouncements, and educational planning. People whose minds are already made up do not need to think about something that is obvious" (pp. 256–257). Smith explains that "sounding out words" interferes with a reader's ability to decode text. According to Smith, people who ascribe to "sounding out" as their primary reading strategy "must be shown that (1) sounding out is a handicap, not a help, to reading; and (2) there is a better alternative" (p. 256).

This generally accepted and unquestioned description of reading as sounding out focuses children, parents, and often teachers on reading as a decoding process that silences discussions of reading as a means of understanding and examining the world. As Cummins (1994) reports; ". . .the public focus and apparent political commitment to improving the ability of students (and adults) to 'read the word' represents a facade that obscures an underlying structure dedicated to preventing students from 'reading the world' (p. 296). As Bernardo Ferdman explains, reading is not just about mastering a set of skills, but is one aspect of literacy which is situated within larger societal norms and beliefs:

Becoming literate means developing mastery not only over processes but also over the symbolic media of the culture—the ways in which cultural values, beliefs and norms are represented. *Being* literate implies actively maintaining contact with collective symbols and the processes by which they are represented. (p. 188, emphasis in original)

Becoming literate is not just learning to read the words on a page but being able to understand and manipulate words and letters in culturally valued ways, "Successful literacy must not only have the 'right' grammar, but the 'right' values, beliefs and attitudes" (Gallego & Hollingsworth, 2000, p. 7). Thus successful literacy involves adopting dominant ways of being relative to literacy tasks encountered in school and society. Reading is one dimension of literacy and is part of a practice that involves analysis of the world as well as mastery over symbolic media and particular beliefs and attitudes; it cannot be reduced to sounding out. The reading behaviors of children in this study challenge the dominant discourse of reading as sounding out since they exhibit complex and integrated strategies to make sense of text.

FIGURED WORLDS: DISCOURSES IN ACTION

Holland et al. (1998) utilize the concept of "figured worlds" to explain how people operate in daily life. They explain that the worlds that we view ourselves to be operating within are historically and socially constructed. We understand these worlds to be populated by particular types of people and we recognize particular issues as being significant or insignificant based on our understandings of the world. Our figured worlds are constantly constructed and reconstructed through our identification of significant events and actions in daily life, our evolving understanding about how and why things happen, our interpretations of new experiences based on those that came before, and our predictions about how particular events will occur in the future. Within figured worlds, people's actions and identities are not predetermined by social and economic contexts. "People's identities and agency are formed dialectically and dialogically in these 'as if worlds'" (Holland et al., 1998, p. 49).

Dominant discourses operate in the figured worlds of people; generally accepted and unquestioned ways of being and knowing inform the figured worlds we inhabit. In my data, there are clear examples of people operating in figured worlds that feature dominant discourses. These dominant discourses are played out despite their inaccuracies. Consider the words of Ms. Weston as she assisted her daughter Tiffany with a challenging word.

Tiffany (*reading*) : I can see the flowers. I can see the bee [the word was
    dragonfly].
Ms. Webster: No, sound it out. What is that? (*Ms. Webster points to the picture
    of a dragonfly on the page*).
Tiffany: Dragonfly

In this brief example, Ms. Webster tells Tiffany to "sound out" the word and then immediately directs her attention to the picture to help her successfully solve the word. Within Ms. Weston's figured world the dominant discourse of sounding out is part of her understanding of reading ,which she accesses even as she draws her daughter's attention to other sources of information.

In a second example, Ms. Holt demonstrates the strength of negative assumptions about urban parents when she challenges her own words, spoken during the initial phase of the research project. When her son Bradford was in first grade, Ms. Holt explained to me why she felt that he might be having difficulty with reading:

> Like when I was coming up and we could go outside this time of day
> and just play and you know not worry about someone coming by
> in a drive-by, didn't have to worry about gang [war-]fare. All these
> different things. You know it was kinda, I felt secure. I don't know if
> he [Bradford] feels safe when he's out there or not. You know what
> I'm saying? I don't let him go too far but I'm just saying when he's
> away, I don't know how does he feel? Safe? Home or not, I don't
> know if that has an effect on him, some learning abilities or not.

Three years later, when Ms. Holt read these words not knowing that they were her own, her response surprised me:

> I don't know, the lifestyle of this person [who is speaking], you
> know. It [her lifestyle] might have a lot to do with the child's ability
> to read, you know. What kind of lifestyle is going on there? Parties
> every night, you know. And late getting up and you have all day
> then you don't have time to sleep, you don't have rest, you know.

The possibility that the child's learning difficulties in reading were related to the violence within the community was not discussed and Ms. Holt immediately suspected that the parent was the culprit. Holland et al. (1998) explain that the cultural worlds we inhabit are "populated by familiar social types and even identifiable persons" (p. 41); Ms. Holt has accessed an identifiable type of person as the speaker of these words and has explained the quote with that type of person in mind. We all do this as we inhabit figured worlds that include categories of people and roles they are expected to play. According to Holland et al., the identities we assume are related to the figured worlds we inhabit.

Finally, the work of Holland et al. (1998) reminds us that although we inhabit figured worlds in which particular types of people and events are understood to exist and that we are affected by the expectations and the routines that are part of those worlds, we are not predisposed to particular ways of being. People in all social contexts have the capacity to act proactively within their worlds: "Human agency may be frail, especially among those with little power, but it happens daily and mundanely and it deserves our attention" (p. 5). Agency taps our generative capacities by building on collective meanings and social relationships to explain and act on the situations we experience. Alternative discourses grounded in people's experiences can be the impetus for acts of agency.

In the following chapter, I present two dominant discourses related to education. The first is a discourse about paying attention in school that explains the learning difficulties of children while maintaining faith in children's abilities. The second, a discourse about the benefits of high-stakes testing, is both voiced and challenged by parents in this study and reflects parents' faith in their children's abilities and their hopes for equity and social justice.

Chapter 2

Two Dominant Discourses: Paying Attention and High-Stakes Testing

It is important to realize that the parents and children in my sample are not dupes who are fooled by dominant discourses because they are unintelligent or ignorant. Dominant discourses act on all of us, including educators. In my initial study, I discovered that my teaching colleagues and I ascribed to many dominant discourses about the children we served and their families; these discourses are challenged by the families in this study. In contrast to dominant accounts that lament the lack of reading material in urban households, I learned that families did have books and did care about their children as readers. Many of the parents in this sample were avid readers themselves: Some read magazines, others read novels; one preferred American history and another read science fiction.

Dominant discourses also exist in reference to schooling and literacy. Graham Nuthall (2005) explores the cultural routines and myths that infect our understandings of teaching and learning. He maintains that mythologies about academic ability as a stagnant quality that some people possess, the idea that learning occurs within simple teacher-to-student interactions, and the assumption that engagement automatically results in learning are all flawed beliefs. Jane Baskwell (2006) makes similar claims about literacy. She maintains that generally accepted cultural norms surround literacy. These include shared understandings about the nature of literacy (e.g., reading is a means to employment and economic prosperity), the role of effort in learning to read (e.g., people who do not read well do not try hard enough), and being a good reader (e.g., good readers are focused on print and sound out words). Within figured worlds dominant discourses define ways of understanding teaching and learning, but these dominant understandings are often challenged by people's experiences and the complexities that accompany social phenomena.

Dominant discourses are often challenged. Some dominant discourses are directly challenged by the stories that participants tell. Others are challenged by people's actions (e.g., discourses that surround sounding out words). Others are not challenged by participants but by the inability of the discourse to explain the complexity of activities such as learning and reading. It is important to recognize that dominant discourses can serve purposes for the people who voice these discourses; both of the dominant discourses explored in this chapter challenge deficit views of children and raise possibilities for equity and social justice.

This chapter explores two dominant discourses that I encountered when speaking with my former students and their parents: paying attention and high-stakes testing. Both of these discourses operate within the figured worlds of people in this study. While on the surface these discourses contribute to cohesive and coherent understandings of the world, when examined closely, disruptions and tensions are revealed.

PAYING ATTENTION:
"THEY PROBABLY DON'T LISTEN TO THE TEACHER"

When I asked my former students why some children have trouble learning in school, most mentioned paying attention.

Author: Alicia, how come some kids in your class have trouble learning to read? How come some kids have it kind of hard?
Alicia: Because they probably don't listen to the teacher.

Bradford: They don't pay attention when the teacher's telling you stuff.

Javon: Because, I think 'cause they don't pay attention in class and stuff like that.
Author: Anything else?
Javon: They don't never try. That's it.

Author: Why did you get a bad grade in reading do you think?
Marvin: I don't pay attention to reading. And sometimes I don't even be in reading [class].

Author: What does um Deantha do? What do you think she does when she reads that makes her such a good reader?
Jermaine: She don't keep her eye off the words she don't look at nobody

like this (*Jermaine's eyes dart to his left and right*). She just keep her
eye on the words. She pays attention. At-ten-tion (*spoken loudly and
deliberately*).

My former students associate school and reading success with paying
attention. They maintain that their own reading and learning successes,
as well as those of their peers, are contingent on paying attention. References to attention recurred throughout interviews with both children
and parents. This dominant discourse places the responsibility for learning on students and assumes a direct relationship between attention and
learning. This simple formula suggests that if children pay attention, the
learning will result.

There is a comforting logic that surrounds dominant discourses about
attention. When children and parents describe attention as the critical
dimension of learning, they challenge deficit views of urban children by
maintaining that there is nothing wrong with the children; cognitively
and intellectually the children are capable and competent and they
would learn if only they would pay attention. The logic expresses faith
in the capabilities of children and posits children's learning difficulties on
distractibility rather than biological or cultural deficit.

However, there is a darker side to this simple formula. Citing attentional issues to account for the academic difficulties of children places
blame on families since parental failings are often assumed to be responsible for the inattentiveness of children. Thus the accountability of schools
and teachers for the academic performance of children is lessened, and
individual children and their families are deemed responsible.

I suggest that the relationship between attention and learning is complex and nuanced. Learning theories that simplistically correlate learning
and attention reflect traditional, "banking models" of education (Freire,
1986) in which the teacher fills the students with information. The
student is depicted as passive during the learning process; attention is the
only required action. Paying attention is assumed to allow information to
pass into children's brains in an osmosis-like process.

"If You Had Listened and Watched Instead of Looking Around"

In this study, parents also subscribe to dominant discourses about
attention. Simplified models of learning circulate freely and generally
remain unquestioned. Like their children, parents often associate school
success with paying attention. I am not suggesting that the parents in this
study are ignorant or naive; I suspect simplified models that confound
learning and attention permeate across socioeconomic and cultural
communities.

When Jermaine complained about the amount of work his teacher had assigned in class during one of our interviews, his mother, Ms. Hudson, admonished him, saying that perhaps if he had been attentive in the first place he would not have needed to do so much classwork: "You know what? If she didn't do that maybe if you had a listened and watched instead of looking around. Your reading would have been much better. Your math would have been much better. See, she was getting you prepared for third grade. "

Ms. Hudson attributes her son's difficulties to attention rather than ability. Jermaine's reading and math would have been "much better" if he paid attention. As evidence that teachers are not immune to these simplified, dominant discourses, I found myself voicing this same discourse during an interview. When Jermaine's mother chided him for not paying attention, saying, "Jermaine, will you pay attention," I heard my own voice on the tape saying, "Hey, no wonder you're having trouble learning to read." My not so funny teasing reveals the power of this cultural model. Despite my teaching experiences and theorizing about learning, I still automatically and routinely accessed this dominant discourse about attention that conflates attention and learning.

Parents are comforted and reassured when they see their children beginning to demonstrate the ability to attend to learning tasks.

Ms. Mason: I told him, I said, "I'm so happy to see you can read long books now."
Mr. Sherwood: He's trying so I got to give him that. He is trying. You know, he's focused on mainly learning.

It appears that parents and children share great faith in the power of attention. Attention is assumed to equal learning and thus is the key to children's success in school.

"Friends and Talk"

Parents often describe other children as threats to their child's ability to attend to school tasks. Ms. Hudson reports that the teachers monitor Jermaine's social activities and move him away from children who distract him from learning: "They be on top of things. They call me [if he] act up in school. Don't they? (*She looks at Jermaine who is sitting nearby*). . . . He get with the wrong crowd and they have to separate them." Ms. Hernandez reports that Jasmine is doing well with her reading but that she is overly focused on her friends: "You know how it is, friends and talk." Ms. Burns agrees; she reports, "The reading's not the problem. It's the following through or following the steps after the reading. . . I have an understanding that all of the fifth graders are having trouble with that [staying focused]." Mr. Sherwood explains that children need to maintain focus on learning despite the distractions of peers:

> You knows what's going on here. He knows the people he's got to deal with in life. He knows the kids he has to deal with in school. 'Cause some of the people in school, they come to school with [issues]. . . . And they go, "Marvin, you've got to do this," and "Marvin, you've got to do that." He don't focus on that.

"It'll Make Him Focus Better"

Although peers are often viewed as a threat to every child's ability to pay attention in class, for two of the students in this sample, attentional deficits were identified by teachers as a particular problem, possibly contributing to their learning difficulties. These two had been or were in the process of being classified as having an attention deficit condition; both are African American and male. Questions concerning the overidentification of African American boys as exhibiting attention deficit or attention deficit with hyperactivity disorders have been raised by many researchers (i.e., Davison & Ford, 2002).

The parents in this sample describe attention as critical to learning. They want their children to be able to pay attention and believe that this attention will enhance their learning. As Marvin's grandmother, explains, "He's a slow learner and he got this medication. And that'll make him focus better and then that way, he'll probably be able to do the work better." Jermaine's mother shared with me a report from the school psychologist that recommended an attention deficit screening. She had completed the paperwork from the school, and school personnel had forwarded the papers to Jermaine's doctor and were awaiting the doctor's recommendation. She seemed comfortable with the pending diagnosis.

Some research with African American educators and parents have described attention deficit as a socially constructed phenomenon that reflects the experiences and cultural beliefs of particular communities and that parents and professionals in African American communities are often reluctant to accept the attention deficit disorder diagnosis for their children (Davison & Ford, 2002). This reluctance is attributed to concerns that range from a general distrust of the school system to a perceived lack of cultural awareness on the part of White educators, or concerns about drug addiction. Neither Ms. Sherwood nor Ms. Hudson raised these issues; rather, it was their emphasis on the importance of their child paying attention in school that guided them to consider medication.

"Catch the Child's Attention"

Despite the power of the dominant discourse, parents challenge this discourse about attention when they recognize the role teachers and teaching situations play in children's propensities to pay attention. Parents describe this happening in two ways. First, teachers must contend with large numbers of children and must remain attentive to all of them. If a teacher does not attend to particular children this inattention can negatively affect the student's learning. Mr. Sherwood explains that it is the teacher's responsibility to remain attentive to the entire class despite large numbers of students: "Focus on everybody, you know, the whole thing. You've got 35 students. . . a good teacher to me [is good] because they focus on every child, the whole class, you know. . . Because everybody in that class is important for that day." Christy's foster mother, Ms. Ross, agrees:

> I don't know, but sometimes I think that maybe and I know they have a lot of kids in the classroom. So, sometimes I think they don't pay enough attention to the children, but then that's a lot of kids to have in your room. Sometimes they have anywhere from 25 to 30 kids in a room. And that's so hard too. But, I just feel if you're a teacher, that's what you're there for.

Student attention is contingent on teachers in a second way; teachers must "catch the child's attention." There is a propensity to view children's attention as something that is floating out there and ready to be "caught" by a resourceful teacher. I asked Ms. Horner about what she felt made a good teacher. She responded: "Things that make a good teacher, I think patience. . . understanding. . . being able to catch the child's attention so that that child will want to learn." Ms. Mason explained that a good book can also have this power over Javon: "Sometimes he'll get some book or something and it catches his attention. And he would say, 'Ma, I want my book. What happened to my book? I want to read it.'"

Complexities of Attention

The parents and children in this study tend to rely on dominant discourses that associate attention with learning. Focusing on attention situates the responsibility for learning with children and teachers and turns a blind eye to the quality and depth of classroom learning experiences. This focus on attention removes our gaze from nuances of instruction, where the reasons and purposes for attending reside. Issues related to accessing and using information are silenced, as are purposes for learning.

The issue is not whether attention is important; attention is a significant factor in learning. Vygotsky (1978) argues that attention is a critical first step in learning and explains that unlike animals, children can "evaluate the relative importance" (p. 35) of elements within a perceptual field. To Vygotsky, attention incorporates not only what a child experiences at a particular time but also the child's past and future as the child attends to reference to ongoing activity. Vygotsky explains that attention involves more than just an ability to recall what was witnessed but also an ability to synthesize the past and present for the purposes of making sense of the present moment. Thus attention involves more than children behaving in class, watching the teacher, and participating in activities.

Suzanne de Castell and Jennifer Jenson (2004) explain that we all learn to give "illusionary attention" (p. 387). *Illusionary attention* maintains social interaction without true attention commitment of the attendee. De Castell and Jenson make an appeal for a more "self-conscious, accountable, and ethical communicative practice" (p. 392). Our focus on attention should not be limited to the need for educators to gain and maintain attention, but rather on developing attention structures that will enable children to engage with new material and utilize that material relative to their intellectual and personal lives. Many other variables, beyond paying attention, are involved. The teacher might be teaching something the child already knows or presenting information that the child is not prepared to learn. The teacher may be giving directions to children about how to complete worksheets and pages of math computation; attention in that situation may not involve new learning. Learning does not result from the automatic transfer of information from one brain to another (Freire, 1986, Nuthall, 2005). Learning is contingent on a range of factors—from providing experiences that are appropriate for particular children to engaging those children in thoughtful, active, stimulating, and critical learning experiences. Attention alone is not enough.

Simply paying attention does not assure us that learning is occurring. Children need to identify appropriate salient elements within a field and have the requisite background that is needed to make sense of those elements. Marie Clay (1998) uses the term *awareness* to refer to "being able to attend to something, act upon it, or work with it" (p. 42). For Clay, the term *awareness* captures the nuances of attention that involve not just perception but the child's ability to integrate new information with existing understandings. As she explains, telling the child information is not sufficient. The performance of outward signs of attention such as watching the teacher or performing the motions of a particular task will not necessarily lead to learning. She offers the example of a child learning to read: "In learning to read it is essential to know where to attend and in what sequence, and how to pick up different kinds of information" (p. 65). Learning involves not only paying attention but attending to the proper things and integrating them into existing networks of information and activity. As Clay (2001) reminds us, children may attend to things that the teacher does not expect. Attention alone is not sufficient; children must attend to the right things in the right ways.

Richard Lanham (1994) maintains that in complex settings, such as classrooms, students must develop "attention structures" that help them to manage and make sense of the massive amounts of data that they encounter. These attention structures enable them to establish the relevance of information to various spheres of their lives and attend to information accordingly. Lanham suggests that attention that leads to learning helps us to sort through, identify, and access critical information

Graham Nuthall (2005) explains that teachers believe their teaching is successful when they observe that their students are actively engaged; they ascribe to "the commonly held belief that if students are engaged most of the time in appropriate activities, some kind of learning will be taking place" (p. 920). For example, "it is not enough to say that a student learned because the student was busy reading a book unless you also identify what the student was reading and how that content related to what the student already knew" (p. 917). Nuthall describes reading as one of many ritualized behaviors that exist generally unchallenged in classrooms and advises teachers to become aware of ritualized behaviors that are assumed to lead to learning.

Ascribing to discourses that equate attention with learning serves purposes for parents and children. When poor grades and learning difficulties are attributed to attentional issues, the innate abilities of students remain unchallenged. It is about the child's willingness to participate rather than his or her intrinsic competence. As the comments of parents reveal, attention and learning also have to do with teachers and their ability to engage children. Once again simplistic discourses are challenged by a set of complexities that involve teachers as well as children and by proxy their parents. It is apparent that issues related to a child's ability to translate attention into learning can be traced not only to the child's current teacher but to prior teachers who were responsible for helping the child acquire requisite knowledge, the development of a sense of relevance for the content to be learned, and an engagement with school constructs and materials.

HIGH-STAKES TESTING: "I THINK IT'S GREAT"

As an experienced classroom teacher and a Reading Recovery professional, I recognize the value of high-quality assessments that involve
observations of children engaged in authentic reading and writing activities. I understand very clearly how the results of careful assessment can
be used to design instructional programs to support children as literacy
learners. The new wave of standardized testing, however, is problematic
and difficult to translate into educational practices. Rather than providing
valuable information to improve instructional programs for children, the
results of these tests are used to punish schools, teachers, and ultimately
children who occupy poor and diverse communities. Thus I was intrigued
when Mr. Sherwood, Marvin's stepgrandfather, voiced enthusiastic
support for the new testing system adopted throughout the state: "I think
it's great. I think it's real great. They could get them prepared for the next
test. . . so they [teachers] can know what's going on. . . . [If it were] left
up to me, a teacher or head of the teacher program, I would have [a test]
every 3 weeks to keep the parent informed." Mr. Sherwood believed that
the new testing system would ensure student learning and keep teachers
and parents informed about students' progress.

Mr. Sherwood's words echo the official ways of understanding testing practices. The official discourses on testing make numerous claims to
justify the use of these tests:

- Harder tests will raise academic achievement for all students.
- Tests can determine whether or not children are meeting
  educational standards.
- Tests will keep parents informed about their children's progress.
- High-stakes testing will eradicate the performance gap among
  various groups of students.
- Schools with high numbers of students who do poorly on tests can
  be targeted and reformed.

Mr. Sherwood's positive views about high-stakes tests are not merely
his personal views; his opinion reflects official rhetoric that appeals to his
interest in Marvin's acquiring a high-quality and equitable education. In
the state where this research was conducted, the Grade 4 English Language Arts (ELA) test was first implemented in 1999. It was 2 years after
I taught the group of first-grade students described in this book and my
former students took the ELA during either the second or third year of
its inception.

"She Passed All of Them"

As I began the fourth- and fifth-grade interviews, I asked the parents about how their children had done on the fourth-grade ELA test. Knowing the low passing rates for students in my district, I expected to hear parents report that several of my former students did not pass the test. I was surprised.

Ms. Johnson: He [David] did well. He did well on it. I don't remember the score but he did well.
Author: And the teacher had mentioned that to you?
Ms. Johnson: Yes. Yes.

Ms. Rodriguez: She [Alicia] took all of her tests and she passed all of them. I'm like girl, right on cue.

Mr. Sherwood: He [Marvin] did good on that. It shocked me. It did. It shocked me. It really did. It really shocked me.
Author: So, you saw the scores? They came home?
Mr. Sherwood: Yes, I did. I did. It really shocked me.

Mr. Sherwood's excitement about Marvin's test score contradicted information he had shared just a few minutes earlier in the interview. Mr. Sherwood had shown me Marvin's fourth-grade report card. His grades were mostly Ds and Fs, and Mr. Sherwood suspected that Marvin had been "passed through" to the next grade, not deserving the promotion. As we looked at Marvin's report card, Mr. Sherwood remarked, "Come on now. Is that passed through or what?"

A few weeks after this interview I was granted consent from Mr. Sherwood and the other parents to access their children's ELA scores. I discovered that, unbeknownst to their parents, Marvin, David, and Alicia had all failed the ELA test.

A lack of clarity involving test scores was not unique to these parents. Despite the hype surrounding the state tests, the yearlong preparation for the tests, and the public reporting of each school's scores in the local newspaper, parents were unclear at best, and at worst misinformed, about how their own children scored on the test. In this district there is no policy regarding the notification of parents about students' test scores. Some parents I spoke with assumed that their children had passed the test because they were not notified otherwise. Other parents assumed that if their child failed the state tests they would not be promoted to the next grade. As Ms. Burns explained, "You would assume if they failed [the State test], that they would be held back." This was not the case for Marvin, David, or Alicia.

Mr. Sherwood made a strong argument in favor of testing. He suggested that frequent testing would allow both teachers and parents to "know what's going on." He maintained that regular evaluation would keep teachers focused on what needs to be taught and keep parents as well as teachers informed about students' progress. Mr. Sherwood adopted a dominant discourse that associates testing with accountability. However, the promises associated with high-stakes testing have not been fulfilled. Giving the ELA test did not ensure that parents were informed of their children's progress. Thus, while Mr. Sherwood adamantly supports the tests, these tests have failed to fulfill their promises to children and families.

"Don't Discourage Him"

I encountered mixed messages that extended beyond the reporting of test scores. Ms. Holt supports the use of tests on the one hand, but tells a contradictory story about her son, Bradford, on the other. Ms. Holt was distraught at the conflicting messages she received from the school about her son, but she maintained that the tests were "good" because they help teachers to monitor students' progress. "I see [them] test all those kids and see where they belong. That's good. That's right there, I don't have any problem with that." However, she was distraught about the conflicting messages she received from the school about her son's achievement and felt that decisions based on test scores were devastating to Bradford.

Despite being a special education student, Bradford was expected to take the same tests as the other children in his grade. While he brought home As and Bs on his daily work, his report card indicated that he was failing the fifth grade. Apparently his report card reflected his progress relative to grade-level standards and tests; no concessions were made for his special education status:

> [The tests are good] but in the meantime don't discourage him.
> You know what they should [have] two tests. If you [are] in a
> special class give me [something different], you know different from
> whatever it is than when you're in a regular class. They're not in the
> same class so why give them the same test? If you're going to give
> him a fifth-grade test, put him in the [regular] fifth-grade [class].

Despite Ms. Holt's frustration with Bradford's report card, she claims that the test itself is not the problem. It is the disconnect between his grades on classwork, his report card, and the test scores as well as the effect failure has on her son that worries Ms. Holt. She describes an interaction with her son, "He's worked so hard and he comes in [asking], 'Mommy, am I doing better?' [Based on] this report card, I don't know."

Other parents shared their concerns about the effects tests have on children. Ms. Hernandez worried that her daughter was being moved on to the next grade despite her struggles in school, and that the tests were not correcting this problem: "I'm still wondering why [she was promoted to sixth grade] if she's not standing up to fifth grade...[in sixth grade] they have more [difficult] problems. It's just like she's going to be more behind. But well you know how they [school decision makers] are."

Ms. Burns is concerned that by the time children reach fourth grade that it is too late to prepare them for the test and that the current testing practices place a lot of pressure on fourth-grade teachers and students: "It is like it is too late in fourth grade to try to teach them all this stuff. It should have been taught from day one. But first grade teachers can't do it. The second grade teachers can't do it, and she's [the fourth-grade teacher is] supposed to play catch-up."

While urban parents, like many other people, often accept dominant discourses about the benefits of testing, the parents in this study present stories that reveal dangers associated with these same tests. Mr. Sherwood and Ms. Hernandez are disturbed by their children being promoted to fifth grade. Ms. Holt is concerned that Bradford will be discouraged by the results of his test score. Other parents expressed concern about what the tests mean for students and teachers.

"Sometimes They Get Mad"

During that second interview, I asked the children about taking tests. Their stories challenged the dominant rhetoric of increased academic achievement as an unproblematic and logically obtainable goal. Some children reported that the tests were too long or too hard; other children described the ways the tests affected the classroom community. Alicia offers a classroom scenario that positions the teacher as blaming the students for not doing well on tests. I asked Alicia what happens when children do not do well on tests:

Alicia: The teacher just yell at you.
Author: Really, she yells at you?
Alicia: If we, if the whole class, like half the class they fail their test, she will yell.
Author: Why do you think she does that?
Alicia: Because (*imitating the voice of a teacher*) "It's a shame."

Alicia's words bring to mind a vision of a frustrated teacher standing before a class of students and telling them what a shame it is that so many of them failed a test. While Alicia's story tells of frustration and anger expressed by a teacher, other children report that testing angers children.

Author: What happens when you don't [do well on a test]?
David: I am mad.
Author: Do you get mad?
David: Sometimes I have to take it [the test] over by myself.

Author: What happens when they [children in your class] have trouble on tests?
Christy: Like if you doing the test, they have trouble and they [the children] act mean. . . if they don't know the answer, they will try to ask somebody else.
Author: And then what happens?
Christy: They get in trouble.
Author: Yeah. What happens if they take the test and they get a really bad grade on it? What will happen to those kids?
Christy: When they go home, their mom or dad will get mad.

Author: What happens when kids don't do well on tests?
Javon: Sometimes they get mad. . . . . They bother other kids.

David, Christy, and Javon all use the word "mad" to describe the ways children, teachers, and parents react to poor performance on tests. They say that kids "act mean," "get in trouble," and "bother other kids." The children's association of anger and aggression with testing challenges official stories about testing that argue for a logical and scientific approach to school improvement.

However, anger is not the only response children report to the test. Some children suggest that surrender is a common response among their peers. I asked David about what happens when he has to take a big test:

David: You can't always give up because some of the kids do that.
Author: Really? What happens when you give up?
David: Um, well, forget it. The test is over.
Author: How do you know some kids give up?
David: Because my, in the second-grade class, kids just didn't want to do their tests and they got 40s and 60s.

The children in this study describe classmates becoming angry and giving up. However the experiences of my former students, like the voices of the parents in this study, remain unrecognized and unheard. Anger, frustration, and the temptation to just give up are silenced beneath misplaced calls for equity.

Dominant Discourses and High-Stakes Testing

Initially, when Mr. Sherwood and other parents voiced dominant discourses about testing, I was confused. The parents spoke of their hopes for equity and academic possibilities. While these tests promise equity and quality schools for all children, recent critiques of testing programs suggest that testing is a means to document the failure of public schools while creating privatized schools and mandated curriculum that benefits educational publishing companies. Using testing to measure school success benefits the testing industry. Too often, when the words of children and parents challenge dominant and official understandings about testing, they are dismissed as individual and personal accounts. The stories of parents and grandparents, children and teachers, are discounted as being subjective, situated, and singular.

Dominant discourses about testing appear logical and natural. As Norman Fairclough (1989) argues, discourses dominate when the meanings of words and situations become "naturalized" and discourses are accepted as truth and remain unquestioned in the public sphere. Naturalized discourses around high-stakes testing are apparent in official accounts, such as in the following report on accountability in the No Child Left Behind legislation:

> Under the act's accountability provisions, states must describe how they will close the achievement gap and make sure all students, including those who are disadvantaged, achieve academic proficiency. They must produce annual state and school district report cards that inform parents and communities about state and school progress. Schools that do not make progress must provide supplemental services, such as free tutoring or after-school assistance; take corrective actions; and, if still not making adequate yearly progress after five years, make dramatic changes to the way the school is run. (U.S. Department of Education, 2003d)

To parents in urban communities, these promises are enticing. Parents want their "disadvantaged children" to be able to compete with more privileged children. They want supplemental services and high-quality schools for their children. No Child Left Behind legislation claims that the methods they espouse are "proven" based on "rigorous scientific research" (U.S. Department of Education, 2003c). This is a compelling promise.

As Fairclough (1989) explains, commonsense assumptions are questioned only when things go wrong in people's lives or when there is a significant gap between the dominant discourse and a person's lived experiences. This is the case for my former students and their parents. No Child Left Behind legislation (U.S. Department of Education, 2003b) does not address the problem of parents being misinformed or uninformed about their child's success on high-stakes tests. While No Child Left Behind requires that states and districts produce "annual state and school district report cards that inform parents and communities about state and school progress," it says nothing about reporting individual students' scores to parents. This legislation does not address Ms. Holt's concerns about her son's grades and the expectation that he should take the same test as other children despite sitting in a different classroom and learning different material. It does not address Ms. Burns's concerns about the pressures that are placed on teachers and children, and it does not recognize the children's anger when they are subjected to frustrated teachers and state-imposed tests.

However, the promise of these claims has been challenged. As George Hillocks (2002) explains, while the tests promise to be scientifically based and attempt to convince citizens that they are demanding and rigorous, the new high-stakes tests are actually political mechanisms that politicians use to garner support. If tests were truly challenging, these tests would be a political nightmare: "If the testing program really is rigorous, it is likely to reveal weak performance, a disaster for any politician claiming education as his chief priority" (p. 151). Despite the high failure rate among my former students, Hillocks explains that the tests given in the state in which this research was conducted are actually lax in the expectations they set forth for students and in the ways they are graded.

In the voices of parents and children, we hear the beginnings of a critique of dominant discourses about testing, grounded in their experiences. Testing practices have negative effects on children and families, leaving parents and children struggling to make sense of testing policies that promise equity but deliver failure.

CONCLUSIONS: REREADING DOMINANT DISCOURSES

The dominant discourses presented in this chapter are just two of the myriad of dominant discourses that we carry with us as we operate within our figured worlds. While we are often unaware of these discourses, they act upon us and upon our thinking. Some dominant discourses are directly challenged by the words and stories of participants in this study;

for example, when parents speak about urban families and testing they tell contradictory stories. Other discourses are challenged by people's actions, as when they talk about sounding out words but actually use other strategies while reading. Some discourses remain powerful and are only challenged in minor ways; paying attention is the responsibility of the teacher as well as the child. The dominant discourses presented in this chapter prey on the dreams and desires of parents. Discourses surrounding high-stakes testing and paying attention challenge deficit views of children and promise equity, yet the stories told by parents belie that those promises and remind us of how discourses act upon us even as we challenge the discourses we encounter.

Chapter 3

Proximity and Distance: Marvin's and Jermaine's Stories

I asked Marvin if his teacher in fourth grade treated him unfairly; he responded with hesitation:

Marvin: I don't know. Sometimes a little.
Author: What did she do that wasn't fair?
Marvin: She skipped me when I started to read and I get mad.
Author: Oh, why did she skip you?
Marvin: I don't know.

Marvin is not sure if he is treated fairly by his teacher but he knows that he gets angry when his turn to read is skipped. Being skipped at reading may have nothing to do with Marvin being African American, male, or his reputation at the school as a troublemaker; but then again, it might. As Holland et al. (1998) explain, the worlds that we view ourselves to be operating within are historically and socially constructed. Social interactions in the past have taught children lessons about fairness, turn-taking, acceptable behavior, and the meaning of school tasks and these experiences along with the experiences of friends and family members contribute to the figured worlds that children and parents inhabit. Students, like all people, understand their figured worlds to be populated by particular types of people—teachers, administrators, parents, and students—and that these roles are further delineated into categories that include difficult students, good students, fair teachers, mean teachers, and uncaring administrators. Existing categories are flexible and can be amended; new roles and ways of being are possible. Within figured worlds particular issues and events such as homework, test scores, and behavior are understood as significant or insignificant. The fairness of one teacher and being passed over in reading group are minor events that gain meaning when they are echoed in other interactions positioning not only the people Marvin encounters but also positioning Marvin as a particular type of student.

The figured worlds of students are constantly constructed and re-constructed based on children's evolving understandings about how and why things happen, their interpretations of new experiences, experiences that came before, and children's predictions about how particular events will occur in the future. Within the figured world of school, students' identities are formed dialectically and dialogically as they act and interact with others (Holland et al., 1998).

On the pages that follow, I present the stories of two boys, Marvin and Jermaine; their stories illustrate how the identities of children as learners and as readers are constructed within complex figured worlds. The data suggest that the identities of children in classrooms are complex, fluid, and fluctuating as the children move between and across contexts assuming various roles and positionings. These stories expose identity construction as a complex and multilayered negotiations that involves sets of congruent and conflicting experiences. Students experience both proximity and distance to school, compliance and resistance, and share warm and antagonistic relationships with teachers. I propose that during these late elementary school years my former students are involved in an ongoing process of continual construction and reconstruction of themselves as students and as readers relative to home, school, siblings, and peer expectations and relationships. The chapter concludes with an analysis of the stories and connects Marvin's and Jermaine's experiences to theoretical constructs related to identity.

MARVIN'S STORY

Marvin is 11 years old and in the fifth grade. Since before he was my first-grade student, Marvin and his sister have lived with their grandmother and her husband, Mr. Sherwood. Marvin sat and listened while I interviewed his stepgrandfather, chiming in occasionally to clarify or contradict what was said. Marvin had grown. In fifth grade, Marvin towered over my 5-foot frame and immensely enjoyed standing next to me and comparing our heights. Marvin's grandfather reports that Marvin now wears glasses but was not wearing them for the interview. Despite Marvin's size, there is a quietness about him. He answered my questions politely and thoughtfully but rarely became animated or excited. On a few occasions, he interrupted his grandfather to offer his own account of an incident. At one point Marvin was told to go upstairs and get his baseball trophy; he came right back with it. Another time he was asked to bring his report card. His marks were almost all Fs.

Marvin had failed first grade the year before he was in my class. During his first year in first grade he had been removed from his parents' home by social services and his grandparents became his legal guardians. Apparently his mother and father were struggling with drug addiction and legal problems. Mr. Sherwood often remarks on how far Marvin has come since he moved in with them: "He came a long way from where he came from." He says that despite the challenges he is proud of Marvin's progress and that Marvin is basically a good person. Mr. Sherwood explains that when they go out in the community and see homeless people and other people in need, Marvin often expresses his desire to help.

When he was in first grade, Marvin had a very close relationship with his older sister who was in fifth grade; she had taken care of Marvin while they were living with their parents and continued to look after him in first grade by picking him up after school and relaying messages to his grandparents. Marvin's stepgrandfather has worked at the same job since Marvin was in first grade; he cleans up chemical spills associated with photocopier machines. His grandmother is on disability.

Marvin had not been retained since first grade but his grandfather felt that he should have stayed in fourth grade. He feels that his fourth-grade teacher promoted Marvin just to get him out of her class. Mr. Sherwood explained, "She passed him through." He shows me his report card which is mostly Fs, stating, "He didn't deserve it, I mean it was terrible. [She] just passed him right on through. . . . I said, 'What's this?' That ain't no report card." Mr. Sherwood reports that Marvin spent most of his fourth-grade year in the principal's office.

Marvin's grandparents are pleased with his fifth-grade teacher and report that she keeps a close eye on him. Mr. Sherwood explains, "She's got to get results. He got to learn more because I think he lost a lot in fourth grade. . . . I think he lost the whole fourth grade."

Marvin has recently started taking medication for attention deficit hyperactivity disorder (ADHD) and is currently in the process of being evaluated for special education services. Although Marvin was receiving speech services since kindergarten, he is now going through the Committee on Special Education to get additional academic assistance. While his grandfather believes that Marvin is functioning as well as other children his age, his grandmother explains that "he needs more than one teacher" and that there are too many children in the regular classrooms. So far he has not been classified with a learning disability; his grandfather attributes his nonclassification to the expense involved in providing these services and cites financial difficulties faced by the school district.

When I asked Mr. Sherwood about Marvin's attitude toward reading, he replied, "He don't like to read," and explained that "he gets bored." Despite his lack of enthusiasm toward reading, Mr. Sherwood reports, Marvin reads "pretty good" and reads to his grandmother every night.

When asked about his favorite books, Marvin instantly mentioned *Goosebumps* (Stine, 1992–1997) and *Nate the Great* books (Sharmat, 1972–2003). His grandfather chimed in to tell me that he also likes to read *Pokemon* books (Michaels, 2000–2004). When I asked about the books that he is reading in school, he reports that he does read chapter books in class but that he forgot the name of the books and what they are about. He mentions borrowing *Junie B. Jones* books (Park, 1993–present) from the school library. Marvin recalls the books he reads at home and those from the school library but assigned books are forgotten.

Based on my past knowledge of Marvin as a reader, I was surprised when at our first interview Marvin identified himself as one of the best readers in the class with the exception of his friend Charles. Marvin explained that he and Charles sometimes read together in the school cafeteria. He states that they read mysteries and that Charles's mother, who works in the cafeteria, helps them with difficult words. However, as the conversation continued, Marvin reported that both he and Charles got Fs in reading last year. Marvin explained that Charles was "just playing around" last year and that his own F was due to his not really liking to read. He added that "usually last year I was to be down in the [principal's] office all the time" because he would "talk back" to his teacher. Like his classmates in the initial phase of this study (Compton-Lilly, 2003), Marvin associates being a good reader with being a good "reading partner" while actual school reading proficiency is ignored. Marvin's identity as a reader involves contradictory positionings that lie between personal and social reading practices and school-assessed reading abilities.

Marvin reports that his teacher allows him to choose topics to write about in class. Marvin writes "scary stories." I asked if his friends also wrote scary stories and he reported that he didn't know and that they did not read their stories to each other. When I asked Marvin to write a story for me he wrote in an awkward cursive about an event that had occurred at school:

> One day i got in a fight in school in ~~a i got in~~ the next day i brige som [*bring some*] beack [*bleach*] in ~~a~~ i got loge tenen [*long detention*]. then i got a prvit true [*private tutor*].

Marvin and his grandfather both described this incident. It is a story that surfaced on multiple occasions. For Marvin this is an important story and it took considerable effort for him to record this brief description on paper. Marvin struggles with writing; basic mechanics and spelling are problematic. The awkwardness of Marvin's script and the multiple cross-outs reveal his frustration with this task.

When I asked Marvin if he needed any help with his reading, he nodded but provided no details. He paused for a moment, perhaps thinking, and answered, "I just think I need help with my reading." He describes doing "round robin" reading in class:

Marvin: I have to read a whole paragraph.
Author: And then what happens?
Marvin: (*pause*) Sometimes I mess up on the words.
Author: What does your teacher do when you're done reading the
    paragraph.
Marvin: She calls on another person.
Author: And they read the next paragraph?
Marvin: (*nods*)
Author: And what do you do after everyone's had a turn?
Marvin: She start back over with me.

Interestingly, he believes that the school social worker, whom he sees regularly to address his behavior problems, helps him the most with his reading at school. He also explains that his grandmother helps him at home. Mr. Sherwood confirms this report:

Doris has really been on him about his math, reading. . . . Yeah she
has, man, she's on him like nothing [you've ever seen]. I'm serious.
She's been on him like this, "You got to do this." You know and
she be on him first thing he hit that door. He think he gotta do his
homework. And she be on him on that homework. It's good to me
. . . she say um, "Where your homework at?" [Marvin answered:]
"Don't worry because I been keeping it in school." You know 'cause
he don't want to do it. [She] say, "Don't try that stuff with me.". . .
She's not no fool. . . She be on him, I mean 100% on that kid right
there. (*Mr. Sherwood points to Marvin who is sitting nearby smiling at his
grandfather's description and nodding his head.*)

Over the course of the interview, Mr. Sherwood offers several reasons for the difficulties that Marvin has faced in school. First, he explains that Marvin is regularly sent out of class to the principle's office for misbehaving in class. This was a serious problem last year in fourth grade. When Marvin visits the office, he sits in the detention center. As Mr.

Sherwood explains, when the child goes down, the supervisor ignores the child. Mr. Sherwood explains that they call this a "time-out" program. Appealing to my experiences as a teacher, he asks in a loud voice that seems to be grounded in his frustration and incredibility, "Do you think that works?" I explain that removing one child may enable the teacher to teach the other children. Mr. Sherwood acquiesces, but argues that you end up with 30 kids going "bizzerk" in the time-out room. He says, "Come on now, if you put animals in cages now, I mean come on. Well, to me, I don't think it works."

Mr. Sherwood also cites the need for the school principal to become more involved with children who are experiencing chronic difficulties in school. He talks about Dr. Perez, the new assistant principal who is a young man of African American and Hispanic heritages:

> He's got to get more involved with the kids though. That's what I
> have to say, you got to get more involved with the kids and see what
> the problem is with that. You know I understand about you're bright
> and young, smartness and stuff, but he's got to get more involved
> with the kids. You know 'cause the kids they're coming in, got a lot
> of problems down there.

Mr. Sherwood makes this same comment about the teachers at the school stating that they need to spend time with the children, talk with the children, and become familiar with the issues that the children are facing. Mr. Sherwood maintains that developing strong personal relationships with children is essential for children, like Marvin, who bring "a lot of problems" to schools and classrooms.

Finally, Mr. Sherwood argues that the schools must offer extracurricular programs that interest children. He offers karate as an example:

> If they had a karate program, Marvin would love it. . . . Softball,
> sports that kind of stuff he do not like. . . . He won't get into that.
> But if you do something like that karate program or something like
> that you get into that, he'll love it. . . . He's very active he'll just go
> around and he'll be boom, boom, boom. . . . It can be something like
> about five people in the room, he'll love every minute. He'll love it.

Families with financial means provide these experiences to their children. Middle- and upper-class children who struggle in school often have opportunities to excel in other areas. Poor children generally do not have these opportunities. Too often difficulties in school are not counteracted with successful experiences that provide children with alternative identity positionings. In urban communities, special programs come and go; they are often temporarily funded by grants or require long-term commitments from parents and community members that are often difficult to maintain in an economically volatile community.

Marvin complains to his grandmother that his teachers do not show him how to do the work that he brings home for homework. His grandmother reports that Marvin often calls a telephone tutoring service that the local teacher's union provides for students: "He'll say 'They told me to do this and I don't know how to do it. And then they didn't show me how. How am I supposed to do it? If you don't show me how to do it'. . . He'll come home, and he'll call Dial-Assistance and he'll talk to them two or three times."

When I asked Marvin about his report card grades in reading and writing, to each query he reported getting "a bad grade." When I asked him why his reading grade was not good, he said, "I don't pay attention to reading. And sometimes I don't even be in reading." He explained, "I be in the bathroom or I be out of the classroom." He continued, "I go to speech or with the social worker." As noted in Chapter 2, Marvin does not attribute his low report card grades to a lack of ability; he blames them on not paying attention and being sent out of class. Marvin appropriately presents himself as bright and capable despite low report card grades.

Thankfully, this year seems to be progressing better than last year. He has a teacher that he gets along with and is spending less time with the principal:

Author: Why do you think things are going good?
Marvin: I stay out of the office.
Author: How is this year different than last year?
Marvin: (*pause*) I don't get in too much fights this year.

Mr. Sherwood agrees that fifth grade has been a better year for Marvin. He explains that Marvin has asked for a bicycle and because Marvin is doing better in school he is considering the purchase: "He likes to ride around. Let him escape a little bit you know and mellow his mind out."

Mr. Sherwood talks about how difficult things are for Marvin: "He tries so hard you know. And then, sometimes he's like, 'I failed.' And he gets mad when he failed." Despite everything, Marvin does try to do good things and please his grandparents. Over the past year, the family has faced a particularly difficult situation. Marvin's older sister, who was 16 at the time, left home and has been living "on the streets" with an older man. Mr. Sherwood explains that this has been a difficult situation for Marvin who was very close to his sister, "'Cause he don't want to talk bad about her. The only thing he said that [is] bad about her is he'll say 'Oh she's a bad girl.' You know. Or he'll say 'She shouldn't do that' and stuff." Mr. Sherwood worries that this situation could have a negative effect on Marvin. "We don't want it to get him the risk [of leaving home and being on the streets], and also he seem like sometimes he [could] get on the path [that his sister is on], that he want to do the same thing."

Fighting was a big issue for Marvin during the first part of his fifth-grade year. At the first interview, Mr. Sherwood noted, "We've got a lot of problems in the area with the kids around here." I asked, "What kind of problems?" When Mr. Sherwood started to answer, "Well mainly, you know kids like to um. . . ." Marvin blurted out the end of Mr. Sherwood's sentence, "Fight!" Mr. Sherwood agreed stating that they fight "a lot."

Mr. Sherwood described the incident that occurred during the previous school year that Marvin had described in his writing.

Mr. Sherwood: Marvin and this boy got in a real serious fight. You know. Marvin got a little—you know those little spray bottles there you know? And he uh put some uh. . .
Marvin: (*chiming in*) Bleach.
Mr. Sherwood: Usually Grandma checked his bag every morning. He didn't tell me nothing about it. I didn't know what was going on you know I got home 'cause I worked the night shift. So, he took it to school. Right. So I got the call right, and he didn't spray no nobody like that, right (*checking to make certain that I understand that he did not spray anyone*)? So. . . I had to go down there. So, [I] talked to [the principal] that was a serious charge.

Marvin's rendition of the story, recounted below, highlights his reasons for bringing the bleach, the fact that he did not use the bleach, and the punishment that resulted from the incident:

I got in this fight one day and the boy's brother jumped in and punched me in my face. So, I brought the bleach to school 'cause, to protect myself because he said he was going to get his brother and his other brother to jump me. And I ain't sprayed or nothing but the teacher smelled it and she thought it was hairspray, but it was really bleach. And she called [the vice principal] and [the principal]. At the end of the day . . . they called my grandfather. And, and I got in trouble real bad. And I couldn't go outside for a whole month.

The incident had serious effects on Marvin and his family. Marvin was suspended from school until after a hearing was held at the district's administrative building. Crime investigators were involved and the meeting was audiotaped. The school's principal, Mr. Williams, and Marvin's teacher were there; they both testified that Marvin had been getting beat up almost every day and that he was preparing to defend himself. As Mr. Sherwood explained, it was good that the teacher and the principal defended Marvin since the committee was considering sending Marvin to an alternative school for troubled youth.

During the 3 weeks when Marvin was suspended from school, he was provided with a tutor. Mr. Sherwood describes this time as "beautiful":

> Just like clockwork. Come right down here, had his book ready, sit back down there on there, I mean she was on him. She looked, she remind me of a nun. I'm serious. She doesn't let him get distracted, I mean 'cause there was one day (*Mr. Sherwood starts laughing as he talks*) I came in here I was you know, and no TV's no nothing, no noise and stuff like that you know. But she told me afterward why she's like that, right. And she sat right [there] for 2 hours. Marvin learned more stuff by her [than in school]. . . . There ain't no distraction at all. I mean, he sat right there for 2 hours, she sat right there and everything was beautiful.

Mr. Sherwood was thrilled with how Marvin responded to the tutoring situation, but he was very disappointed when he discovered that the school was not informed about how well Marvin had performed in tutoring: "She [the tutor] got it right and she good, but you know what? They [school personnel] got no reports of what he did with her. I can't understand that. Do you understand that? Every day [she tutored Marvin]. They didn't get no reports for all that? I couldn't believe [that]." Throughout the interviews, Mr. Sherwood repeatedly praises the school principal, Mr. Williams. Mr. Sherwood explains that he really "got involved" with the students. Following Marvin's incident with the bleach, Mr. Williams invited Marvin to open the parking lot gate for the teachers each morning. As Marvin excitedly reported to me, "I'm a public safety."

Mr. Sherwood reports that the new assistant principal, unlike Mr. Williams, does not relate well to the children. Mr. Sherwood explains that Mr. Perez is perceived by the children and their parents as discouraging children:

> [He'll make a] remark [to] Marvin and then Marvin will carry it back in the house and tell us what's going on. . . like if he [Mr. Perez] was going, "You can't make it in this world. You ain't going to do this 'cause you got to do it this way." . . . I mean this child is just trying to

make it hisself. He's trying to grow up and do [it right]. That's putting him down. And then he don't like that. That's the only problem he got going down there. . . . They [the children are] going to keep that right in their head.

Having heard many administrators and teachers, including myself, lecture children on their behavior, I know that it is very easy to slip into threats of what will happen if particular misbehaviors continue. While teachers view these threats as warnings coming from people who care, children may perceive these threats of impending doom as statements about their worth and value. Thus good intentions aimed at helping children see the consequences of their actions may be interpreted by children and their parents as statements about children's worth and potential.

Thankfully, Marvin also seems to be developing some very positive relationships with his peers. He explains that he enjoys going on field trips because "I get to hang out with my friends a lot." When asked what he and his friends like to do, Marvin lists playing basketball, talking about scary movies, and watching the SuperBowl. He tells me about a new movie that he and his friends are looking forward to seeing. He even tells me "there's like a group of kids that I know and we study together" at school. If they ask his teacher, she will let them work together and "study." "One person be the teacher and we get a sheet of paper. [We act] like it's the test and then we got to write all this stuff down and then we look in the book and see if it's all right." In some instances Marvin's positive relationships with others present possibilities for Marvin to identify with school. His improved relationship with his current teacher, the cooperation he demonstrated with his home tutor, and his reading of books in the school cafeteria, all suggest spaces that could lead to positive school experiences.

When I gave Marvin a brief reading assessment, he was able to read and comprehend text at the fourth-grade level. Unlike his grandfather's report, Marvin reports that he did not do well on his tests this year. He states that his reading grade went down and that he got 50s and 60s in other areas. When I checked to see if he passed the fourth grade ELA test, I discovered that he had failed. All of these experiences, positive and negative, are contributing to the person that Marvin is becoming.

Mr. Sherwood reports that Marvin sometimes gets frustrated with school and will say things like, "I'm dumb." But Mr. Sherwood disagrees:

I guess the main thing to me that is they tell you one thing down
at the schools but he's so smart when he here. He speaks real good

and everything, and they [school personnel] tell me how you can't speak [and need speech classes]? He be usually going for hours on me. . . sometimes he'll like to sit down there and look at um TV and . . . then I say it [a word] wrong, right? And then he'll know it right quick. He'll say, "Hey Grandpa, that's wrong." I says, "You're right." He's like, "You don't even know." So he's telling me. And he gonna be [OK], he's on the right track.

As Mr. Sherwood explains, "He's been hanging in there." He explains that Marvin wants to be a police officer because he wants to help people.

Marvin's story is full of contradictions. He forgets the assigned books he reads in school but speaks enthusiastically about his home reading and library books. He struggles to follow rules in school, but wants to be a police officer. He describes himself and his friend as good readers despite failing grades which he blames on not paying attention and being out of class. Later in the interview, he describes studying with his friends in school. Marvin's relationships with school personnel vary drastically. He has the support of the principal and his current teacher, but other administrators and teachers are viewed as unhelpful. For Marvin, being a good reader is caught up in his relationships and peers; it relates to the relationships he shares with reading partners in the classroom and roles he plays relative to not only the teacher and the school expectations she conveys but also his peers and their expectations. It is not simply reading accurately or being able to retell accurately what was read; reading competency occurs within a figured world that involves peers, relationships, and purposes for reading.

Marvin inhabits a complex figured world, and in response to that complexity we see him assuming various positionings at various times and in various situations. As we read Marvin's story, we read of a child who is torn between competing identities. He wants to be a good student, but struggles to meet school expectations, academically and socially.

JERMAINE'S STORY

At the time of the second interviews, Jermaine was 10 years old and in the fourth grade. Jermaine presented himself as soft-spoken and polite. He had gotten a bit chubby since first grade and had just started wearing glasses during the past school year. He explained to me that he repeated second grade because of his reading and because his grades went down.

Jermaine's father is retired and his mother is currently on disability.

Ms. Hudson had two unsuccessful back surgeries in the past 9 months to address chronic back pain. Despite her continued discomfort she is considering going back to work as a nurse in a nursing home. Ms. Hudson is happy to be living in a single-level house, but sometimes appeared to be in pain during our interviews. When I arrived for the second interview, she was lying in a darkened room but seemed happy to talk despite her apparent discomfort.

Jermaine has attended two schools since first grade. During the year of this study, he was identified as having a learning disability and was provided with tutoring services, as I mentioned in the Introduction. His mother showed me some papers from the school that described Jermaine as having a "disorder of written language."

When asked what books he likes to read, Jermaine identified nonfiction books. He listed books about animals, tornadoes, science, spiders, airplanes, bears, and fire hydrants. He even reported reading the dictionary. He also mentions several book series that are animated on television including *Arthur* (Brown, 1976–present), *Clifford* (Bridwell, 1963–present), and *Blue's Clues* (1996–present). Jermaine explained that the best thing about reading was "just looking at the book," but that his teacher tells him, "You gotta read like three pages," which he does not like. When asked if he liked to read he responded "just a little." His mother shook her head and reported that he "hates" reading. Jermaine, who was sitting nearby, disagreed:

Jermaine: No, I don't.
Ms. Hudson: Yes, you do. When I be trying [to tell you] Jermaine go upstairs [and] put your "Math Made Easy" tape in and when you get through do some reading, what you do? What, what attitude do you be giving me? What you be doing?
Jermaine: (*growls playfully at mom*)

Jermaine explained, "I just don't like reading at home 'cause I don't like to read at home. I like to read at school." Ms. Hudson did not appear convinced.

When I asked Jermaine about his favorite writing topics, his response was noncommittal and less than enthusiastic: "I just be writing things like I just be writing good, like this. I be looking at the books. [I write the] name of the book, read it, write something about the girl and the dog or the. . . (*unclear mumbling, Jermaine's voice fades out*)."

I asked Jermaine to read some graded word lists and text passages. Based on these assessments he appeared to be reading at approximately a

second-grade level. Consistent with his classification as having a disorder
of written language, Jermaine's writing is notably immature for a child in
fourth grade.

1. I like gym becase I like to run.
2. I like art becas I like to pant [*paint*] and grow [*draw*]
3. I like my techer becase he is nice.
4. I like my frind beacaase They is not mene [*mean*] to me.
5. I like my mom becas she is nice to me and my frind.

This writing sample contains some blatant errors such as three different
spellings of the word "because" and extremely simple sentence structures. Being a contrived writing assignment created for the purpose of
this research project, this writing may not reflect Jermaine's true abilities;
however, I was concerned.

Despite Jermaine's difficulties with reading and writing, he resists and
resents the help that the school provides. His Individualized Education
Plan (IEP) entitles him to 3 hours of reading resource help each week.
Jermaine does not like being taken out of his classroom for this special
attention.

Author: So do you think you need help with reading?
Jermaine: (*pause*)
Ms. Hudson: Yeah.
Jermaine: I don't want no help for reading.
Ms. Hudson: Yes, you do. You need it.
Jermaine: I need to try by myself.
Ms. Hudson: Well, you still need help, that and you try. You need help.

While Ms. Hudson describes what Jermaine "needs," Jermaine focuses
on what he "wants," and he does not want extra help in reading. Jermaine wants to try to become a good reader by himself. Jermaine explains that his classroom teacher helps him by sending him to the back
table to read by himself. His mother agrees that this helps him, "Because
he can't concentrate on the book with a bunch of people around." She
explains that his older sister, who is now in college, was the same way in
school. Jermaine explains:

Jermaine: They should have me do my reading alone. 'Cause I don't be
    sad [when I am alone]. I just be sad at myself because I can't read.
    Everybody pick on me and everything.
Author: They pick on you because you can't read very well?

Ms. Hudson: Kids did me like that too.

Author: Really?

Ms. Hudson: But I got it together. And let them kept on picking. Ignore them and I got it together. They couldn't pick no more.

Jermaine: They do. They call me, right now they call me a four-eyed baboon.

Ms. Hudson: Them only words.

Jermaine: They call me four eyes.

Ms. Hudson: They's the words, don't hurt.

Jermaine: They call me, they call me King Kong with titties.

Ms. Hudson: Yeah because, you know why they're doing that because they're trying to make you not learn. They don't want to learn. That's why they're doing that.

Jermaine is expressing contradictory feelings about being part of the class. His desire to be a good student and learn to read are challenged by the teasing he experiences leading to his requests to be allowed to "do my reading alone." He doesn't want to be singled out for extra help but is also very aware of his difficulties with reading and resents the teasing that occurs in his classroom. Jermaine and his mom agree that his difficulties with reading are in part due to his need for glasses. Ms. Hudson reports that Jermaine's new glasses are helping him. She indicates that Jermaine does not like to wear his glasses and that she would often get calls from his teacher last year because he was not wearing his glasses in school. Jermaine explains that he has to "look at the print" and that his new glasses will make a difference.

Jermaine: Since I got my glasses and um, my mommy just said, "LOOK ON THE WORDS" (*emphasizing each word*).

Author: (*laughs*)

Jermaine: "LOOK ON THE WORDS (*emphasizing each word*) and um concentrate. . .

Author: Mmm-hmm.

Jermaine: And um concentrate on each word.

He explains that his reading is not that good because "I didn't used to pay attention to my teachers. I used to always be talking every time [in class]." In contrast, he describes a little girl in class who he identifies as a "good reader," "She just keep her eye on the words." He later adds, "She don't never be bad. She acts like a student." Jermaine associates being a good reader with keeping eyes fixated on text, good behavior, not talking, and assuming the student role within his figured world of the classroom.

Throughout both interviews with Jermaine, teasing is a serious concern. Jermaine described being teased by his former classmates when he was retained in second grade. Unfortunately for Jermaine, teasing often led to fights. When I asked Jermaine to tell me a story about school he recounted a recent fight with his arch-enemy, Curtis. I have reworded parts of Jermaine's story for clarity and space considerations:

> When I was in fourth grade, me and Curtis got in an argument. He said one word to me and I just yelled out, "Leave me alone fat boy." Then he said, "Your mama [is] one of those quick people on TV." I was like, "Look at your momma she looks like ET with her breast cut. Wait 'til we get outside I'm gonna bust your nose. I am gong to beat you up until you die." He said, "You'll have a bloody nose and everything. I am going to make you cry."
>
> When we went outside for recess, Curtis hit me when I was in the bathroom and I chased him down the hall. I punched him dead in his back and I went in the class and Curtis came back to class. Then in comes Mr. Bates, he writes up everything. Mr. Bates said, "Somebody just punched Curtis in the back" and Curtis pointed right at me. Later when we were dismissed, Curtis told me to meet him outside. I was like "Yeah whatever. I'm not going to fight because I don't want to get suspended."
>
> So I was waiting for the girl from his class up at the park 'cause she wanted to talk to me but she set me up with Curtis. All the people were there and Curtis was behind them. So when I heard them call my name, Curtis jumped out. He jumped out of the crowd. And he said, "Jermaine give me a fair fight." I was like "Who you talking to? I don't want to hurt you," so I turned back my back. I came back, turned around, pushed him, and then he grabbed my hair. He grabbed it so tight it was hurting me and then he had something that scratched me right in my face and on my arm. It was a pin or something like that. I didn't see it. I felt something stinging my face, so he grabbed me, pushed me against the wall. I punched him in his eye and I slammed him and I pushed him up and throwed him into the gate. And he swung at me and I swung at him and I punched him in his mouth. And then his teeth were like this. (*Jermaine shows two of his fingers bent to one side.*)
>
> This teacher tried to break it up and I pushed the teacher and I came back and popped Curtis, in the back of his head. Curtis turned around and tried to land one on my back. I punched him in his teeth again. And then while the teacher was holding me, Curtis slapped me and then I forgot and I tripped the teacher. I jumped on Curtis' back and said a curse word. And I got in trouble. I think it was Curtis's fault.

This story is one of several that Jermaine told about altercations with Curtis and other children during the two interviews. Jermaine explains that he fights "too much" in school. His mother clarified that he fights, "maybe once a week, once every 2 weeks" and that it's been "terrible" since he's been at his new school. Jermaine laments, "Fighting, fighting, fighting, fighting. I don't like fighting."

Jermaine struggles with his identity as a fighter. He explains that he does not see himself as the "type of person" that likes to fight, but explains that people bother him at school. He is torn between being good and defending himself:

> The reasons at my school that I don't like nobody because they like to start shoving me about that they want to fight and everything and I am not that type of person that like to fight. The only time I got to fight when I am by, when I'm on the streets, I got to defend myself. The other thing, I don't like about [his current] school because there are a lot of kids that pick on other people and a lot of kids that pick on me too. And I notice.

He tells his mother and me, "I used to be a good boy," to which his mother replies, "You still is good." Jermaine responds with more accounts of being bullied by Curtis. Jermaine struggles to retain his identity as a good boy despite peer relations characterized by teasing and fighting.

Throughout the interviews, Jermaine tries to make sense of his school experiences both in terms of his personal identity and his identity as a reader. As one section of the interview lapsed into a conversation between Jermaine and his mother, Jermaine displays his efforts to contextualize himself, a struggling student within the larger social field. He explains to her that "Some people don't get As. When they get bigger, when they be in high school they get Bs, Cs, Ds."

Ms. Hudson: Yeah but we don't want you like that.
Jermaine: But I don't know how to get As. I don't. . .
Author: Sure, you do.
Ms. Hudson: Yes, you do.
Author: What do you think you have to do to get an A?
Jermaine: Uh, study a lot.

But what does the simplistic solution that I elicit from Jermaine offer him? He gave me a rote response, "study a lot." Slogans such as "study a lot" or "just say no" are surface solutions but how do those solutions align with the other issues in Jermaine's life? How are they resolved alongside his struggles with Curtis and the other children? What do they mean to a child who struggles with reading and writing? What does it mean to "study a lot," and what types of identities accompany those actions?

As described above, Jermaine's mother insists that he "still is good." Through everything, the phone calls, the visits to the principal's office, the detentions, and the suspensions, she maintains faith in her son. When I asked how reading was going for Jermaine, Ms. Hudson replied, "Still stubborn." Ms. Hudson looked at Jermaine who was sitting nearby and spoke directly to him. "Yes, you're stubborn." From the time Jermaine was my first-grade student, his mother has noted his tendency to be "stubborn." Stubbornness is part of Ms. Hudson's figured world and part of the story she tells about Jermaine as a student. Notably, this story challenges school definitions of Jermaine as learning disabled. While Jermaine's mother is pleased with his special education classification because it means that Jermaine gets additional services, she repeatedly states that his primary difficulties with learning are due to being stubborn, "Actually she [his teacher] said he's a good boy; he's just stubborn." Like the inattentiveness cited by Jermaine, both stubbornness and inattention place blame on aspects of attitude rather than intellectual deficits. Jermaine's potential to learn remains intact.

Although Ms. Hudson recalled that Jermaine was having difficulty with reading when he was in first grade, since then he has attended two other schools. She indicates that at the second school the teachers gave her the impression that his reading was improving, but when he attended fourth grade at another school she was told otherwise: "I got in conference with his teacher, the teacher told me he couldn't really read and I didn't really understand, I couldn't understand that."

At the end of the second interview, I asked Ms. Hudson about her greatest fears for Jermaine in terms of his education. She identified his reading as her major concern. She remains hopeful that his reading will improve in the future and hopes that the extra help that he is now receiving will make a difference. She maintains faith in him and believes that with the additional help "it is going to get better." Jermaine reports that he is thinking about becoming either a man who "works at a car shop" or a "house builder."

Like Marvin's story, Jermaine's story is full of contradictions. He enjoys nonfiction books at school but resists reading at home. He expresses his desire to be a "good boy" but reverts to fighting. He dislikes fighting but feels that he has to protect himself. He blames his difficulties with reading on not paying attention; he is classified as learning disabled, but his mother reports that the problem is his stubbornness. He admits that he needs help with reading but does not like to be taken from his class and asks to be left alone saying, "I need to try by myself." In one school, his teachers reported that he was doing well at school; in another school they said that he couldn't read. Like Marvin, we read of a child who is torn between competing identities. He wants to be a good student, but he struggles both academically and socially to meet school and home expectations.

CONCLUSIONS

The contradictions faced by Marvin and Jermaine occur within figured worlds that have been historically and socially constructed. Their ways of understanding the world include particular roles and identities that people assume and particular issues and events that are understood as significant or insignificant. Dominant discourses, ways of being and understanding the world, circulate within these figured worlds: Attention leads to learning; boys need to defend themselves; not doing well in school will result in failure in life; and reading is getting the words right. These discourses operate at school and home as children interact with parents, teachers, siblings, and peers.

The stories of Marvin and Jermaine reveal that the boundaries between home and school are continuously being drawn and redrawn as students interact with different people in different contexts. In some cases home interests align with school interests. There are places in the interviews where the goals of students, parents, and school personnel align. Mr. Sherwood praises the school principal and his current teacher for confirming Marvin's report that he was getting beaten up almost every day; this confirmation helped Marvin avoid placement in an alternative school. He appreciates his teacher's willingness to keep in touch with the family and the principal's efforts to help Marvin by making him a "public safety." Jermaine's mother supports the efforts that Jermaine's teacher has made to get Jermaine additional services to support his learning; she praises this teacher for "talking them [school officials] into it." Ms. Hudson is hopeful that the extra help in school will help Jermaine become a better reader.

In other instances home and school expectations and explanations are in conflict. During Marvin's fourth-grade year, his teacher was viewed as "just pushing him through" to get him out of her class despite his failing marks. Mr. Sherwood expresses his frustration that Marvin's positive experiences with his tutor when he was suspended from school were not reported to the school. Both Mr. Sherwood and Marvin express their frustration with the vice principal. Similarly, Jermaine's mother expresses frustration that third-grade teachers indicated that Jermaine was doing well with reading, when he moved on to fourth grade in another school she was told that Jermaine "couldn't really read."

Siblings and peers are important players in children's figured worlds. While both Marvin and Jermaine feel the need to fight to establish themselves among their peers, both express contradictory feelings about fighting. Marvin believes that most of his fights are in self-defense and aspires to be a police officer so that he can help others. Jermaine says, "I am not that type of person that like to fight" and "I don't like fighting," despite his mother's reports that he gets into fights "once a week or once every 2 weeks." Both boys have older sisters. Like Jermaine, his sister liked to read by herself at school. Marvin rarely speaks of his sister's leaving and his grandparents worry that he will encounter a similar fate. These stories and others act upon children and are incorporated into the figured worlds children construct.

Marvin and Jermaine waiver between proximity and distance to school, compliance with and resistance to school expectation, alliance and antagonism with peers, and warm and antagonistic relationships with teachers and other school personnel. They love one teacher and reject another. They praise one administrator and complain about another. They describe friendships alongside chronic fighting. Through these complex, fluctuating, and often confusing experiences, my former students are involved in an ongoing process of constructing themselves as students and as readers relative to home, school, and peer expectations. Like the research of Cappello (2006) and Godley (2003), the stories of Marvin and Jermaine reveal contradictions related to literacy and identity and suggest that identities are constructed within socially and historically charged contexts.

Elliot Mishler (1999) explains that "we speak—or sing—ourselves as a chorus of voices, not just as the tenor or soprano soloist" (p. 8). Gloria Anzaldua describes identity as the "clusters of stories we tell ourselves and others about us" (quoted in McCarthey & Moje, 2002. p. 231). Our stories are always situated within social relationships that involve power and positionings. As Mishler explains, stories about ourselves are "produced through our dialogue, coconstructed in the ongoing process of our trying to make sense to each other" (p. 15). Because identities are formed and reformed within particular social contexts the various selves that we present and aspire toward, like the identities of Marvin and Jermaine, are inconsistent and contradictory. Sarup (1996) describes our identities as "full of contradictions and ambiguities" (p. 14). He explains that "every person's identity is a site of struggle between conflicting discourses" (p. 73). Godley (2003) explains that literacy learning is interwoven with gender, race, and class and that subject positions associated with these ways of being affect the ways students perform and interact as readers and writers.

Researchers such as Bartlett (2005), Gee (2000/2001), and McCarthey and Moje (2002) have documented the bidirectional relationship that exists between literacy and identity: literacy affects identity just as identity affects the literacy practices children adopt. As McCarthey and Moje explain, literacy and literacy practices are means for performing particular identities. The identity of a 10-year-old boy who likes football and can defend himself on the playground is played out in particular ways; reading particular types of texts or not reading those texts is one way of playing out an identity. Marvin and Jermaine use literacy to explore various identities that they assume. Marvin reads with his best friend in the school cafeteria. He reports that they are among the best readers in the class despite both failing reading last year. Marvin reads horror and detective stories; both align with his male identity. Likewise Jermaine is interested in characteristically male nonfiction subjects: animals, tornadoes, spiders, airplanes, bears, and even fire hydrants; however, he does admit that the best thing about reading is "just looking at the pictures."

School-defined failure with reading is also part of Marvin's and Jermaine's figured world; both children have assumed roles as struggling readers and writers at school. Marvin describes his embarrassment in messing up the words during "round robin" reading and at other times being skipped over when it is his turn to read in class. Jermaine describes being teased by the other children and wanting to read in the back of the classroom by himself. For both these boys, their developing interests in books directly conflict with teachers' and peers' assessments of them as failing readers.

If literacy and literacy practices are means for performing particular identities, as McCarthey and Moje (2002) explain, what are the literacy practices that are consonant with the personal and academic identities that Marvin and Jermaine are acquiring? How does school-defined literacy failure contribute to the identity positionings that are available to these children within their figured worlds of school? For students in school, being literate means adopting and continuing to engage with the words and meanings of the dominant culture. This creates difficulties for students whose backgrounds do not easily resonate with the values, norms, and beliefs of the dominant culture. Marvin and Jermaine are not simply attempting to succeed in school, make friends, learn to read, become young men, or align their school and home lives; Marvin and Jermaine are involved in complex interactions with a range of people who sometimes share interests and agendas and who sometimes conflict with each other. These complex interactions contribute to Marvin's and Jermaine's developing personal and literacy identities.

Nilda Flores-Gonzalez (2002) explains that schools create conditions that channel students into assuming either "school kid" or "street kid" identities by providing or withholding opportunities for children to assume or reject valued school roles. She argues that schools can contribute to students' assuming the school kid role by providing forms of recognition and rewards, fostering close relationships between students and teachers, providing consistent positive feedback, creating opportunities for students to mix school-related identities with other identity positionings, and exploring with students possibilities for social mobility.

Unfortunately, it appears that the developing literate identities of Marvin and Jermaine are not aligned with school expectations and that the identities that both boys are constructing are not valued at school. The situation appears challenging. Frustration, fighting, and negative feelings about their reading abilities appear to be taking a toll on Marvin and Jermaine. Yet, possible avenues that could reconnect the boys with school interests and agendas exist. Marvin reads with his friends in the cafeteria and Jermaine enjoys nonfiction. Both boys express their dislike for fighting and describe their intention to be good. The figured worlds of Marvin and Jermaine include roles and positionings that converge with school and parental goals and sometimes the boys are able to fulfill those roles. As long as children's figured worlds present these positive options and the children are willing to work toward assuming these roles, possibilities exist. However, assuming these ways of being is difficult work and the boys may need support in meeting this challenge.

For both boys, their school and literacy experiences have contributed to the opening or closing of particular doors related to ways of being. Some of these doors involve school success; others involve success in other contexts. Still other doors lead students to assume roles that school and/or community members may describe as less than successful. The challenge for educators is to become aware of the figured worlds that children inhabit and to strive to identify and enable options for children that allow them access to new or previously closed doors while respecting the multiple identity positionings that they possess. McCarthey and Moje (2002) describe the need for teachers to help youth challenge and explore the literate identity options that are available to them. There cannot be binary ways of being: good or bad, school kid or street kid, smart or stupid. More complex and nuanced positionings must be available and supported:

- The identity positions available in school must match the complexities that children experience: tough boys can be readers, and doing well in school does not mean abandoning friends and family.

- Children who have experienced failure must be provided with ways to use school for their own purposes and to learn the lessons that they believe will be relevant and valuable.
- Educators must create successful experiences for students that offer new gateways and reopen doors that previously were closed to children.
- Children must be helped to critically examine the roles that occupy their figured worlds and challenge the limits and the boundaries of those roles to conceptualize new hybrid ways of being.

Children's figured worlds offer continual possibilities for success in school and beyond, but educators must work to highlight the relevance of school learning to the children we serve and this will require change from teachers and the educational system.

The work of Cappello (2006), Godley (2003), Hawkins (2005), and Lewis (2001) demonstrates that young children are developing identities as readers and writers and enacting those identities in classrooms. Awareness of identity development in young children relative to literacy is critical as we attempt to help children become literate and see themselves as people who can use literacy to achieve their personal goals. The words of Marvin, Jermaine, and their parents suggest that identity work is ongoing and that there are opportunities for children, with the help of significant adults, to explore possible personal and literate selves. The stories of Marvin and Jermaine offer insights into the complexities that accompany identity construction and provide us with complex and multifaceted accounts that defy simple explanations. Children, like all people, continually construct and reconstruct their figured worlds. As educators we must recognize the existence of continual reconstruction and the hybridity of children's experiences so that we can participate in the opening of doors and the creation of possibilities rather than the reification of limited ways of being and being literate.

Chapter 4

Gender and Schooling:
Alicia's and Jasmine's Stories

Author: How is the school year going for Alicia?
Ms. Rodriguez: Oh, it is going good. It's just she got to stop running her
    mouth. (*Author and Ms. Rodriguez laugh*)
Author: Uh-oh, has she been a little talkative in school these days?
Ms. Rodriguez: Alicia [has] always been talkative.

Gender expectations play a critical role in the figured worlds of children;
they affect the ways children relate to school and in ways schools and
parents view children. Alicia's talkativeness is presented as a problem,
a problem that is routinely associated with preadolescent girls. In this
chapter, I explore the cases of Alicia and Jasmine, two of my former students who shared a propensity toward talk and social activity. While both
girls attended Rosa Parks School in first grade, Jasmine is now attending
a school on the other side of the city and the girls no longer know each
other. Despite their physical separateness, their cases suggest continuities
alongside intriguing differences that promise to shed light on how these
girls construct and reconstruct their ways of being and understanding as
they move across space and time.

Manifestations of gender expectations were evident in the cases of
Marvin and Jermaine (see Chapter 3). Their reading interests and their expressed need to defend themselves, even if it means fighting and breaking
school rules, can be read as manifestations of masculine expectations. Yet,
as demonstrated in the previous chapter, gender roles and expectations
are tightly interwoven with a range of other issues and experiences, de-
fying simple explanation and analysis.

ALICIA'S STORY

When I first returned to visit Alicia and her family, it was the summer before Alicia entered fifth grade; she was 10 years old and lived with her mother, four older brothers, and a little sister. Her stepfather was no longer living in the home. Alicia, her little sister, and an older brother whom I had taught many years earlier met me at the door, and Ms. Rodriguez greeted me as I came into the house. The room was rearranged but the contents were the same with the exception of two new ceiling fans that spun as we talked. We quickly settled into familiar, comfortable conversation. Ms. Rodriguez and I sat on the sofa and talked; the girls remained nearby throughout the interview. Alicia's four older brothers, a cousin, and a friend came in and out of the living room throughout the interview organizing money and transportation needed for a trip to the movie theater to celebrate a birthday. Alicia's mother was still working at a day care center, but had plans to open her own day care within the next couple of months.

Ms. Rodriguez reported that Alicia was doing well at Rosa Parks Elementary School. She explained that Alicia was going into fifth grade and was "right on schedule." However, as I noted in Chapter 2, Alicia's school records indicate that Alicia had failed the fourth-grade state ELA test; Ms. Rodriguez's assumption that Alicia is doing well is understandable as parents in this district are not routinely informed about their children's scores on state tests and often assume that their children passed the tests unless they are notified otherwise. When asked about her report card, Ms. Rodriguez reports that Alicia had recently "brung her scores up because at first she was going like this"—Ms. Rodriguez motioned downward with her hand. She explained, "But I had to get Alicia in order and get on her and cut out some of her activities. . . . Alicia went from failing to a B." At this point in the conversation, Ms. Rodriguez turned to Alicia saying, "See, I knew you could do it. It's just a matter of you buckling down and doing what you've got to do."

When I went to visit the family the following February, Alicia had just brought her report card home. Ms. Rodriguez again commented on her grades. Apparently her science grade went up from a D to a C+ but her reading grade went down from a B to a C+. Ms. Rodriguez was not satisfied with these grades. "It's bad on her part because her teacher said that she knows Alicia is a very capable young lady but she likes to run her mouth." When Alicia was in first grade, she made consistent progress in reading. She ended the year reading fluently at a second-grade level. When she was in fifth grade, Alicia was able to read nonfiction text at her grade level with excellent accuracy but answered only half of the questions correctly.

Ms. Rodriguez reports that most everything is the same this year as it has been in past years for Alicia. As the conversation that opens this chapter illustrates, Ms. Rodriguez worries that "Alicia [has] always been talkative." Unlike in first grade when Alicia described herself as "just talk[ing] a little and then read[ing]," Alicia explained that now, "I read a lot and I talk a lot and it gets me in trouble." Her mother attributes her social proclivity to her father who she says "loves to talk and make friends."

Ms. Rodriguez says that Alicia was excited about joining the chorus at school and swimming at the community center that is attached to the school as part of her physical education classes. Being on the step team continues to be her primary interest. Ms. Rodriguez was pleased with Alicia's fifth-grade teacher, and Alicia also liked her, referring to her as "ghetto," which, she explained, means she's cool. Her teacher was African American. Alicia says that free time was the best part of school and spoke about "Friday Fun" when they listen to loud music and dance. She also described the party that they had on the last day of fourth grade. She reports that the biggest change since first grade is that now she has more friends.

While Ms. Rodriguez is generally pleased with Alicia's progress in school, she did locate a tutor to help both Alicia and her younger sister with their reading because she felt that they weren't getting enough reading practice at school. She reports monitoring Alicia by reading with her occasionally and tells her, "If you have a problem and if you don't see the words the way you are supposed to, let me know, because I know how frustrating that can be." She reports that one of her sons has a learning disability that the school was unsuccessful in addressing.

By the end of fifth grade, Alicia's enthusiasm for school was low. She reports that school is easy but that "some of my classes get on my nerves like usual." I asked why she thought her report card grades had gone down and if she was getting all her work done. She reported that she tries to do all her work but "When they [teachers] make me mad, I just stop." Alicia first claimed that her teacher "yells for no reason," but then qualified her response saying that she yells "Because I tell people to shut up, because they be dissing me." Later in the interview, Alicia complains that her teacher "don't do nothing. She don't help me." Alicia explained that she only helps the children who are having trouble in school whom Alicia refers to as the "retard people."

Alicia reported that she read a variety of books: "I read chapter books and I read baby books and sometimes I read to my sister. And I read big, big dictionaries." Like her mother, Alicia prefers novels written by favorite authors. She enjoys the *Babysitters Club* books (Martin & Lerangis, 1986–2000). She reports that she has read about eight books from the series. I asked if there were any Black characters in the "Babysitter" books. Alicia said that one of the characters was Black but shook her head when I asked whether this was important to her. However, some of her other reading interests reflect Alicia's African America heritage such as her interest in her brother's book about Martin Luther King and her reading about an African American basketball player. During our second interview, Alicia wrote about reading the *Goosebumps* books (Stine, 1992–1997) with a sense of bravado.

Alicia values independence and views being able to read independently as evidence of being a good reader. Her mother explains that sometimes Alicia is not "sounding out her words" and because of that her brothers sometimes help her. Alicia agrees that being able to "sound out" independently is a criterion for being a good reader: "I read all the time and I practice sounding the words and I read the book and I know how to read. . . and I started reading by myself." She explains that she is getting to be a better reader: "I can read big books and I don't need help from other people." Alicia reports that she does not need help in school with reading because she is "smart." She reports that the English Language Arts test she took in fourth grade was easy although her school records indicate that she failed the test.

Since first grade, Alicia has always been positioned as the "good girl" in the family. Her mother explains, "Alicia has not changed very much. She's still the one if something happens [with her brothers, I'm like], 'OK, what did you do to her? Because I know you had to do something to make her cry.' Because Alicia don't do nothing but stand there and cry." As Ms. Rodriguez talks she directs her words to her younger daughter, Quanzaa, saying, "Alicia is not my problem child. Right, Quanzaa?" Alicia reports that her little sister fights. Mom describes the differences between the two girls, "Quanzaa is more of my active one, that's the tomboy one. She [pointing to Alicia] do just what little girls do. And she [referring to Quanzaa] fights and everything." Quanzaa described an incident that occurred last spring when she was in third grade; apparently she fought with a girl who she felt cheated during a track meet. Ms. Rodriguez says that Alicia is like one of her older brothers, "the one that never got into trouble." Being good has been a theme for both Alicia and her mother as they describe Alicia in school and at home.

At the second interview I asked all of the children to write a story about school as I chatted with their parents. Alicia willingly took her paper into the adjoining room and began to write. However, she clearly attended to our conversation and often contributed from the next room. Her mother and her brothers reminded her several times to stay focused and finish her writing. Alicia begins her writing with her account of talking in school. She blames her talking on a friend getting her in trouble and quickly moves on to step dancing during lunch, which also gets her in trouble.

I read a lot and I talk and it gets me in trouble and this girl name
Tanisha and I be telling her to shut up. Lets talk about lunch time. I
always do my step and my dance to my step and I always like to be
bad in lunch because sometimes it's boring. Let's talk about reading
I always like to read the Goosebumps books because they are funny
and sometimes scary because I don't believe in the things they think
they make kids think they are scared of but not me because I really
Alicia Rodriguez. Let's talk about writing me writing is getting much
much better because I'm starting to write neater and neater as you
can see by my paper and I could really write good in cursive I'm
going to show you. *Alicia Rodriguez.*

She closes her account with information about herself as a reader and
a writer that reflects the questions that I typically ask her during interviews.

Alicia expressed mixed feelings about the books she read at school.
She initially reported that "none" of the books were her favorite, but that
she likes "mostly all of them." During the second interview, she reported
that *Two Under Par* (Henkes, 1987) is her favorite book from school, but
she told me very little about the book when I asked. Alicia mentions other
books; one is called *There's an Owl in the Shower* (Craighead, 1995), but
she cannot remember the titles of the other books she has read. Both the
books she mentions have White male protagonists.

Ms. Rodriguez occasionally reads to Alicia and her little sister, Quanzaa. Quanzaa reports that her mother recently read them a book about
Dr. Martin Luther King that belongs to her older brother. Ms. Rodriguez
complains that the assignments that Alicia brings home from school are
becoming more complex, "Some of the stuff I am looking at I ain't never
had that [in school]." She reports that both the math and the reading
assignments are more difficult. "Before they used to have a list of vocabulary words and you have to make a sentence and try to come up with the
definition, [now] she has to make a story out of the vocabulary words and
in the sentence she is telling the meaning of it [the vocabulary word]."

Ms Rodriguez values teachers who "are going to help" the kids. She
explains, "somebody that's going to go that little extra mile with them."
She describes an incident that occurred last year when Ms. Rodriguez
felt that Alicia was falling behind due to her mother's separation from
Alicia's stepfather. Ms. Rodriguez felt that Alicia needed more help with
her reading. Ms. Rodriguez's request was initially honored by the teacher
who began to send home more reading work. Later in the year, the teacher
stopped sending the work and Ms. Rodriguez found Alicia and Quanzaa a
tutor at the local community center, as mentioned previously.

While Alicia's older brothers were generally in and out of the room during both interviews, they rarely contributed to the conversation. However, when I asked Ms. Rodriguez, why she thought some kids were having trouble learning to read in the city schools, one of Alicia's brothers chimed in, "Teachers don't care."

Ms. Rodriguez went on that she worries about her children's safety in school. "Nowadays you have gangsters [saying] 'You looked at me wrong.' Or 'You done stepped on my shoes'. . . [or they are] mistaking you for somebody else." Her teenage son reported that he did not find his high school frightening "because they got it closed off; they lock the doors." Ms. Rodriguez replied, "I believe it is the people in the school." Initially I thought Ms. Rodriguez meant the other students in the school, but her son caught her intended meaning, "Right, house administrator, substitute teachers." Ms. Rodriguez continued, "Teachers seemed like when I was coming up that they care. Now they seem like they just there for a paycheck." She explains:

They [teachers] want the respect from the kids but they don't want to give that respect. So they want to talk to you all any kind of way and then expect you all to sit back and say, "OK." . . . [They're] kids that are practically grown that is looking at you like, my Mama don't talk to me like that.

She explains that she would put her children in a suburban school, but she "can't afford it. I continued the conversation with Ms. Rodriguez as Alicia's older brothers and cousin chimed in.

Author: Do you think the schools discriminate against certain groups of people?
Ms. Rodriguez: Yes.
Older brother: Yep.
Older brothers and cousin: Yes, yes.
Author: Anyone else [joking]? In what way do you think they do that?
Ms. Rodriguez: Um, my point of view is more or less that if you're White, it seems like you get a better education but a Black person a lot of times they just try to push you through school and which I refuse to have to them push my kids through school.
Author: How do you prevent that?
Ms. Rodriguez: Talking to the teacher because they figure um most of the time the Black kids a lot of them they have a parent that don't care, so you have to actually show them that uh-uh, no, this is a parent that do care.

Notably, Ms. Rodriguez does not position herself as a victim. She reports that her involvement with her children's schools prevents her children from being pushed through school.

In fifth grade Alicia was very excited about being on the step-dancing team. As her sister explained, "She's a stepper." Her brother chimed in, "[She's] captain of the girls' step team." Alicia reports that she belongs to the step team at the community center that is attached to her school and attends practice "mostly every day." She was looking forward to the overnight trips to step show competitions.

While Ms. Rodriguez supports Alicia's excitement about being on the step team, she blames stepping for a recent decline in her grades. She points to Alicia's most recent report card and shows me how her grades have gone down since she was on the team and says, "So she know, if she don't bring her grades up by next quarter, no more step team." Alicia, who is sitting nearby, complains, "I ain't going to be able to go, I want to go to the Step Off [a step competition in the area]." Her mother assures her that all she needs to do is to bring her grades up. Alicia explains that her friend, Tanisha, bothers her every time she tries to do her work, but her mother does not accept this excuse.

At the time of our second interview, Alicia's team was preparing a step routine to music from the movie *Sister Act*. The family had rented the video and it was playing in the background during our interview. While I chatted with Ms. Rodriguez, Alicia and her sister watched and waited for a scene that occurred near the end of the movie. When the video came to Alicia's song everything in the house stopped. The volume on the television was cranked up as brothers, cousins, mom, Alicia, her sister, and I gathered around the small television screen making room for Alicia to perform her steps along with the video. Alicia blushed and self-consciously moved to the music while her brothers and cousins hooted at her moves. The entire family seemed to enjoy the performance. As the song ended, Ms. Rodriguez explained that they had rented the video because Alicia needed to practice. "She has to learn that dance because that's a big one they are doing [for the step show]."

When I asked Alicia about the worst thing about school, Alicia identified fighting. She reported on a boy who lived across the street, who was also in my first-grade class. She says that he fights with other children at school: "He always go to the office. He got suspended and everything." Alicia also told me that she saw Marvin earlier that day in school; he was storming out of his classroom and cursing at his teacher. Alicia reports that no one fights with her in school.

JASMINE'S STORY

When I arrived at the apartment, Jasmine answered the door. She said "Hi" and seemed glad to see me and then immediately ran off to find a neighborhood friend. Ms. Hernandez remarked that friends seem to be the most important thing to Jasmine lately and that Jasmine constantly wants to be with her friends and had recently become interested in boys. Ms. Hernandez is a very pretty woman and she looked much happier than I remembered.

Ms. Hernandez, Jasmine, and Jasmine's younger brother continued to live in the same apartment and in the same housing project that is on the same block as Rosa Parks Elementary School. Ms. Hernandez explained that she was no longer with Jasmine's father and that she has a nice boyfriend. Although her apartment is very close to Rosa Parks School, Jasmine's mother seems pleased that she "got her in" a much-sought-after school located at the city's fringe that has significantly higher test scores than Rosa Parks School and a better reputation in the community. Her mom explains that she took Jasmine out of Rosa Parks School because she felt that the teachers did not have strong teaching skills and that they should have been doing more. She says that Jasmine's little brother is still at Rosa Parks School; she believes that the school has improved and she is pleased with his progress. Before entering her new school, Jasmine spent some time at a charter school but Ms. Hernandez took her out of the charter school due to difficulties with her work schedule. Ms. Hernandez reports that she would love for both of her children to attend a suburban school.

Ms. Hernandez had recently quit her job assembling dry cleaning orders for a local cleaner; she explained that she was planning to "start tomorrow going looking for jobs." She explained that she was having difficulties with a coworker and was seeking a new job that pays at least nine dollars an hour and is considering work in an office or day care facility. She is also thinking about attending classes at the local GED center. She reports reading women's magazines in her spare time. Ms. Hernandez was the only parent who did not complete all three interviews during the first-grade phase and only completed one of the two interviews during the fourth- and fifth-grade phase. Although she always seemed happy to talk when I managed to contact her and was thoughtful and forthcoming in her responses to my questions, she was very difficult to reach despite my many attempts during both phases of the project. Jasmine happily completed both interviews and seemed to enjoy our time together.

We settled in at the kitchen table just as we did when Jasmine was my student. Ms. Hernandez expressed her concerns about the importance Jasmine places on her relationships with her friends. We sat and talked for a long time. When the interview was over, Jasmine had still not returned and it was getting late. I asked if I could I pick Jasmine up on the weekend and take her out for lunch; Ms. Hernandez thought this would be fine.

When I arrived to get Jasmine, she was standing outside her grandmother's apartment building with her brother and grandmother. I had never met Jasmine's grandmother before. She speaks little English and seemed a bit cautious about letting Jasmine go with me but Jasmine's enthusiasm reassured her and Jasmine and I went to McDonalds for lunch. At the end of the interview, Jasmine indicated that she definitely wanted to be interviewed again. I took her back to her grandmother's apartment and watched her walk into the building.

Ms. Hernandez reports that although she grew up in this neighborhood, she is no longer happy here. She says that she would move to the suburbs if she could.

> It changed a lot I mean now. There's more drugs and sometimes
> you walk around and they shooting people and getting in people's
> houses. . . I don't want my kids to go through all that. I don't want
> [them] to see the same thing. . . but you know, you can never say
> that because one day in life they will probably see it too. . . School,
> like I said this school, I don't like it very much. And especially I don't
> know [about] the environment around here. I don't know. I don't
> like it much.

Ms. Hernandez reported that "something has happened since first grade" for Jasmine. She worries that Jasmine is "not standing up to fifth grade where they have more [difficult] problems. It's just like she's going to be more behind. But well you know how they [kids] are." Her mother reports that although Jasmine's reading is fine she worries that Jas-mine's math is not good. She explains that while her boyfriend, her son, and her ex-husband are very good in math, that "mother and daughter's got PROB-LEMS!" Jasmine reports that she likes math although she is not sure if she is good at it. She agrees with her mother that they are alike in terms of their math ability: "My mom could do a problem and if she don't know how, [she has to] take her time but I'm a little like her because I don't have to take my time sometimes, and then but sometimes it takes me that time because I got to try and put it right."

Ms. Hernandez worries that Jasmine's friends distract her from her studies, "You know how it is, friends and talk and... yeah, my god. It's crazy." Ms. Hernandez reflects on her own experiences and worries about Jasmine: "You know how when you're in the teenage life you just want to hang out with your friends and you don't want to be in school. You do all the mess-up stuff that you shouldn't have done. And then you regret it because I regret it so much. I used to love reading." Ms. Hernandez believes that things are changing for both of her children as they move through school. She compares Jasmine to her son, Willie:

> My son Willie he was saying the same thing [as Jasmine] and when she was younger [that he likes school]. First grade and kindergarten and now he likes it but he's like, "It's getting harder." I'm like, "Well, it's not going to be no easier." He's in third grade now. He is such a good student and he works so good at what he does and everything. He makes me proud. . . he's so good. He gave me a good report card. Real good.

I ask how Jasmine's report card was. I was surprised at the answer.

Ms. Hernandez: Jasmine's was good and but she gave me two Ds .
Author: Really?
Ms. Hernandez: And there was one on math and one on science.

Ms. Hernandez expresses confusion about Jasmine's grades. She suspects that "sometimes Jasmine don't like to pay mind, that sometimes their [minds] wander off, sometimes [it's] friends, and talking and she's not paying mind." Yet, at the same time, Ms. Hernandez reports that "sometimes she comes here with tests and she got hundred percent in science or social studies." The discrepancies between daily grades and report card scores leave Ms. Hernandez struggling to make sense of her daughter's progress. "I don't know, it's like I guess she like gets on there [doing well] and then she like falls off or something." Ms. Hernandez also explained that Jasmine is having a "rough time" with her dad's leaving.

Although Jasmine started first grade in the lowest guided reading group, by the end of first grade Jasmine was reading at a beginning second-grade level with excellent accuracy. When I visited Jasmine during the summer between fourth and fifth grade, Jasmine continued to read at grade level, but was struggling to comprehend what she read. She read a fourth-grade story with 96% accuracy but provided a minimal retelling that omitted many important details from the reading. In fifth grade, she read 99% of the words in a nonfiction passage correctly but struggled with the comprehension questions.

Jasmine reports that they do more work in fifth grade and agrees with her mother that the work is getting harder. Despite her low grade in science, Jasmine reports that the most exciting projects in school are science experiments. One involved melting butter in hot water and the other involved metal tuning forks and the vibrations they make when hit on desks.

Jasmine does not like social studies; she complains that it is hard and she has trouble remembering the things she learns. They were studying about explorers and Jasmine was assigned Cortez but says she cannot remember much about him. Jasmine is excited that she is taking French this year but wishes she could take Spanish as well. While Jasmine understands spoken Spanish she is not satisfied with her speaking ability and wants to take Spanish because she does not "know a lot of words."

Although Ms. Hernandez expressed concerns about Jasmine's school progress, she was pleased with Jasmine's fourth-grade teacher. As noted earlier, Jasmine had switched schools twice since first grade and, according to her mother, found herself behind when she arrived at her current school. As her mother explains, "She was way low, yeah, she was lost." She gives credit to Jasmine's fourth-grade teacher: "Her teacher from last year he was great. His name was Mr. Foster. He was nice. He was great. I mean he told me she did a good comeback last year." Ms. Hernandez explains that Mr. Foster did not give up on her: "He kept on and kept [on] and she did it and I like that in a teacher. You know what I'm saying. You know they would send me papers, dittos, [saying] 'This would be good for her.' . . . You know, I like all that cause they're concerned."

While mom seemed pleased with Jasmine's progress last year and was happy that her teacher decided to pass her on to fifth grade, she continues to worry that they might pass her on to sixth grade even if she is not prepared. "But if [for] some reason they want to pass her and she's not doing good I don't want them to pass her." She explained that Jasmine loves to sing and she is hoping that Jasmine will attend the School of the Arts for high school but said that Jasmine has "got to focus on this year" in order to get there.

Jasmine likes her fifth-grade teacher and appreciates her teacher's sense of humor:

> Sometimes when people mess up we start laughing. You know,
> we fooling around, and my teacher she like laughing a lot so, um,
> when we mess up, she just plays with us and she laughs at us 'cause
> sometimes people don't know where they at (*Jasmine laughs as she
> speaks*). One time my teacher was reading, and they're [the kids
> are] reading, and this boy was reading and he was daydreaming and
> when it was his turn to read after me, he didn't know where we

were at, and then he was just starting all over the place and we were all laughing.

Jasmine's light-hearted telling of this anecdote suggests that the laughter was enjoyed by everyone, even the student who lost his place. Instead of reprimanding the child, the teacher made light of the child's inattention. Jasmine describes this teacher as "flexible," allowing children to pursue their own reading interests: "She gives us DEAR [Drop Everything and Read] time so we can read [books we choose]" and "she gives us time to do whatever we need to do."

Jasmine tells me that if the kids are good, her teacher has a party for the class each month. Jasmine explains, "We just do [have parties] 'cause you know we work a lot, and I mean I can't stand [working] without doing things [like parties] because if we work a lot it's too much work for me."

Ms. Hernandez reports that Jasmine reads books that she purchases at the school book fair and "she sits up in her room, sits and reads her books." She has recently become interested in pop magazines: "Now, she likes to read guys like NSYNC and stuff like that." Jasmine confirms this new interest saying that she recently read a Britney Spears magazine as well as others about NSYNC, Just Justin, and the Backstreet Boys. She also mentions an old reading anthology discarded by a former teacher: "I like them books, they're fun to read and the pictures are fun to look at."

Jasmine says that her favorite author is "Judy Blume." She offers a couple titles, "Judy Blume and Her Big Fat Mouth" and "Judy Blume Smells Fishy." Jasmine has confused the author Judy Blume with the character Junie B. Jones (Park, 1993–present), who has a similar-sounding name. She also reports enjoying the *Arthur* books (Brown, 1976–present).

When I asked Jasmine who helps her with her reading, she clearly stated, "I help myself" and explained that she attended a math and reading program at her school. She explained that the program showed her how to read and do things on her own. She explained that they encouraged her to "take it easy on reading" and not get nervous. She says that reading is not hard for her, but when I asked if she thought she was a good reader she answered, "a little." Jasmine spoke about the importance of reading:

> I guess you can pass your grade if you're a good reader and don't have to struggle. And you don't have to practice a lot cause you know how to read very, very, very, very, very good. So, I think reading is fun. Especially the pictures, the words and like, and you give expressions [to the text]. I like giving it expressions. . . . 'cause a book can't talk, you got to talk just like it.

She explains that children who are good readers read all the time, even when they have free time at school. In addition, good readers sound out words when they get stuck.

Despite Jasmine's growing interest in friends and boyfriends and her inconsistent grades, Ms. Hernandez explains that she appreciates her daughter's ability to understand various situations and to address problems in school when they arise; her "comeback" in fourth grade is a notable example. As her mother explains, "She gets it. You know that's what I like about her." Ms Hernandez explains that Jasmine knows when she is behind in school and she can take measures to address the situation. Jasmine also knows when she does well in school; as her mother explains, "She'll get happy. She gets the [way the system works], she does, she's a good kid."

Jasmine is excited about some of the writing she has done this year. Her class is writing "make your own adventure stories." Jasmine's story is about "going to school and having problems with her friends and hating my friends." She lists for me friends she has included in her book. Jasmine explains that they each wrote reports about themselves and smiled brightly when she told me that they were allowed to write these reports in cursive.

When I asked Jasmine to write a story about school she again described all the hard work she has to do.

> In school I work all day and never stop not unless we go to gym or art and computers. I have fun in school. I love to learn a lot but if I have too much work my hand will start herting. I love school but I don't like wakeing up so early in the morning to get dressed for school. I don't like waking up early because it is not enough sleep for me. I have to wake up at 7:30 and I take my bus at 8:15.

Jasmine explained that her teacher reads a story aloud from their basal anthology and then asks questions about the story. When I asked her what books they were reading in school, Jasmine reported that she read a "good book" about a lady explorer but that she forgot what it said. She is currently reading about salmon and said that the book they are reading tells "how they were born and what do they look like when they're born. When they get out of their egg and what color their egg is."

As described above, children in Jasmine's class are invited to choose their own books for DEAR time, a time when all of the children and the teacher read each day. Jasmine proudly explains that she reads alone. She recently read *Cam Jansen and the Mystery of the Haunted House* (Adler & Natti, 1992). She explains, "We get our books and then we read about it and take notes and then we put it in our own words and we take our own words and we got to write in cursive." Jasmine again smiles when she mentions the privilege of writing in cursive. According to Jasmine, her teacher had warned the children against reading "baby" books, and Jasmine laughed telling me that one of the boys had brought a Pokemon book to school. Jasmine explains that her teacher helps her learn to read by having her write these book reports.

Ms. Hernandez helps Jasmine with her reading but only when Jasmine is "in the mood." She says that she helps Jasmine with tricky words and has Jasmine discuss what she reads. Ms. Hernandez reports that there are many times when Jasmine complains that reading is boring. "Now she's getting a little too, oh God. She just like hypes too quick, I mean she's got this attitude that, I don't know. She can be so nice, the person she is and then she changes. So I don't know. . . I don't want to get her upset, 'OK, fine you don't want to read.'"

Unlike Alicia, Jasmine does not mention fighting at her school. In fact she says, "I mostly like everything" about school and "I can't say I don't like nothing." Ms. Hernandez tells me what she tells her children:

Everybody hates classes. When I was younger like you I hated it too. That is the thing that you got to do because that, that's your main priority. You got to finish school. . . I'm not going to force my kids if they don't want to go to college you know. But I will stick by them in every way I can for them to finish at least their high school and you know I want them to have a good career. I don't want them to be, believe me if I can and could afford it I would move away from all of that 'cause it's just not right. It's not right for them especially growing up and then they see... (*Ms. Hernandez's words drift off as she gestures toward the window, drawing my attention to the community outside*).

Like Alicia, Jasmine reports that she did well on the ELA test that they took last year. She explains that they practiced a lot for the test, "We helped each other. Like partners helped each other and we would take the test by ourself like that person give you a test and if you get it right that means that you probably get it right in the test. And if you get it wrong you got to do the problem you got wrong and then go over it a lot." Despite this preparation Jasmine, like Alicia, failed the test.

CONCLUSIONS

Like Marvin and Jermaine (Chapter 3), Alicia and Jasmine are operating in figured worlds that have been historically and socially constructed and bring ways of understanding the world that include particular roles and identities that people assume and particular issues and events that are understood as significant or insignificant. Gender plays a role in the identities that are easily available to children and in determining the events and issues that are considered important. For example, in the figured worlds of Alicia, Jasmine, and their mothers, place shared significance on particular issues and events:

- Both girls mention and enjoy the parties they have at school.
- Both girls and their mothers present themselves as "good girls" who follow classroom rules.
- Both girls appear to be performing on grade level in reading but were recently considered for retention.
- Both girls were described as making a good comeback and improving their grades when needed.
- Both mothers describe their daughters as being exceedingly social.
- Both mothers describe their daughters as being at a challenging age and explain that school interests are not their daughters' primary concern.

Dominant discourses about gender operate in figured worlds acting on both boys and girls. These dominant discourses belie mainstream ways of thinking about and being female. In her classic critique of developmental theories, Carol Gilligan (1982) argued that accepted models of development fail to reflect the experiences of women. Specifically, Gilligan argues that descriptions of development favor logical and linear thinking often associated with masculine thought while devaluing female reasoning processes that often highlight care, relationships, and responsibility for others. For example, as Gilligan argues and the stories of Alicia and Jasmine illustrate, the cultural ideal of femininity is associated with the "good girl." Good girls are characterized as passive, compliant, receptive, gentle, nurturing, expressive, caring, and self-sacrificing, and social relationships are primary. We can see Jasmine and Alicia working to fulfill these female roles.

In school the "good girl" role translates into being a good student: behaving in class, completing work, being quiet, not being retained, not fighting, and obtaining passing grades. Hicks (2002) describes *goodness* as multifaceted. Like the children in this study, the children in Hicks's research associate being good with learning to read and being smart. However, as the stories of Alicia and Jasmine illustrate, they are not always good girls and social interactions are sometimes defined as problematic. These experiences create contradictions that challenge the formula that simplistically equates goodness with learning. For example, in first grade

Jasmine told me she was a good reader because she "don't play" and she "don't hit people." Being a good girl and being a good reader are not separate.

In her study of working-class children and literacy, Hicks (2002) reminds us that reading practices are not separate from other aspects of being: "Reading is part of children's situated histories. . . readers and practices of reading are situated within histories of locality, gender, race and class. Literacy learning is part of these histories, not something that children do as a cognitive task divorced from their lives" (p. 37). Hicks explains that the books children read are not merely about subject matter. Books are about the relations of feeling and valuing that accompany the reading of these texts. The language of books, like all language, is filtered through the social relationships that people inhabit and the ways of being that are expected, valued, and silenced in various social contexts. In this study, Alicia and Jasmine share similarities in their reading practices and preferences:

- Both girls describe the importance of reading independently and sounding out words.
- Both girls celebrate their new skills with writing cursive.
- Both girls speak with enthusiasm about things that they read outside of school but struggle to remember books they read in school.
- Both mothers describe loving reading when they were younger.
- The reading preferences of both girls reflect the reading preferences of their mothers. Alicia reads multiple books from the *Babysitters Club* series all written by the same author, while her mother reads multiple novels written by a favorite author. Jasmine reads teen magazines while her mother reads women's magazines.

Reading independently, developing reading preferences, and mastering cursive are signals of maturity that the girls celebrate. Like their mothers, they position themselves as enjoying reading and talk about the books that they enjoy outside school, although they remain less enthusiastic about the books that are assigned in class.

Alicia's and Jasmine's continuities as readers exist alongside intriguing differences. Alicia talks about the boys fighting at school; Jasmine does not. Jasmine describes interesting writing projects and choosing her own books to read at DEAR time; Alicia does not. Jasmine's mother worries about her math skills while Alicia's mother was more concerned about her reading and the work becoming more difficult.

For both girls, the work is getting harder and it requires more effort. As

Jasmine writes, "In school, I work all day and never stop." Both mothers are concerned that the difficulty of the work may become a problem for the girls. Ms. Rodriguez complains about the complexity of the assignments that Alicia brings home from school. Ms. Hernandez worries about Jasmine's progress in math, citing her own difficulties. Other researchers have documented the tendency for parents and teachers to express concerns about female students when schoolwork becomes more demanding; their fears reflect dominant assumptions about girls' logical (Gilligan, 1982) and mathematical abilities (Walkerdine, 1990) and contribute to the figured worlds that Alicia and Jasmine inhabit.

Dominant discourses about learning define Jasmine's interest in boys and Alicia's talkativeness as potential problems. Their stories suggest that the girls should abandon social ways of being because they challenge school and classroom expectations. This social propensity and interest in forming alliances with peers is one of the dimensions that Flores-Gonzalez's (2002) account identifies as differentiating "street kids" from "school kids" as children move through secondary school. While some of the positionings that accompany being female appear to serve school interests (i.e., not fighting) others are potentially problematic (i.e., talking in class, being a poor math student, having trouble with difficult work).

Female identities are complex and while some dominant ways of being associated with preadolescent girls are perceived as problematic, other ways of being insulate girls from other problems. For example, while both Marvin and Jermaine feel the need to defend themselves physically in school and fighting gets them into trouble, Alicia and Jasmine do not feel pressure to fight, enacting their roles as "good girls" and "good students." As their stories testify, both Alicia and Jasmine have assumed fairly traditional female roles in their schools and homes. Not all of the girls encountered in this study fulfill traditional female roles. In fact, Alicia reports and her mother confirms that her little sister, Quanzaa, fights at school.

Like the boys described in the previous chapter, disjunctures and contradictions exist in the figured worlds of Alicia and Jasmine. Alicia is progressing "right on schedule" in school, but was considered for retention. Jasmine is doing better in school, but her mother worries about her being retained next year. Both girls failed the ELA test and express their ambivalence about the books they read at school. The report card grades of both girls fluctuate. While poor behavior problems beyond talking in class are not issues for Alicia and Jasmine, the social worlds of Alicia and Jasmine are at odds with the expectations of teachers.

In her book on working-class children, Hicks (2002) argues for hybrid spaces that allow multiple and complex ways of being alongside school success. Alicia and Jasmine are already experiencing the need for and appreciation of spaces that welcome multiple ways of being. When the girls read school assigned books about White boys and lady explorers that are far removed from their experiences and interests, they cannot remember what they read. When Alicia gets in trouble for step-dancing in the cafeteria during lunch, she learns about the inflexibility of the school even during noninstructional times. Formal spaces such as these silence social ways of being and the ideas and interests of the girls.

Yet it is essential to recognize that these narrow spaces exist alongside official spaces that invite participation and nurture academic relationships. When Alicia describes her teacher as "ghetto," she recognizes her teacher as "cool," despite her teacher's propensity to yell "for no reason." Her participation on the "step-team" is a notable and prominent success in Alicia's story. In general, Jasmine's experience of school is more positive than Alicia's. Jasmine is often allowed to choose some of the books she reads at school, she engages in interesting writing projects, and she enjoys her teacher's sense of humor. Like the boys described in Chapter 3, the figured worlds of Alicia and Jasmine offer possibilities for school success and spaces that accommodate their ways of being.

The figured worlds of Alicia, Jasmine, and their mothers raise one further dimension worthy of consideration. Their mothers are critical of the schools their daughters attend. Both Ms. Rodriguez and Ms. Hernandez perceive suburban schools as superior to city schools and recognize problems in the communities surrounding their homes. Both worry that their children will get pushed through school without learning what they need to compete in the job market or attend college. Parents reference the underfunded schools and neglected communities where their children are expected to grow and learn.

While both parents bring strong and warranted critiques to the schooling of their children, Ms. Rodriguez's figured world features a particularly powerful critique. Unlike Ms. Hernandez, Ms. Rodriguez has older children who have moved through the school system; she and her sons have experienced teachers who they describe as not caring and are "only there for the paycheck." She watched as one son's learning disability went unaddressed. These critiques contribute to the figured worlds of school and society that Alicia inhabits and provide spaces for agency on the part of children and parents.

The figured worlds of Alicia and Jasmine are clearly affected by their gender positionings, yet they are also characterized by contradiction and fluidity as children assume multiple roles within the figured worlds that are offered. Just as identity construction for the boys in this study is contested as boys struggle to embody multiple and sometimes contradictory ways of being, the girls in this study also experience a range of complex, compatible, and contradictory expectations and experiences across various contexts and within various social relationships that include teachers, parents, peers, and institutions. As Hicks (2002) explains:

> Class relations, gender, and school practices are lived in ways that are fluid, not easily confined to more reductive categories of analysis. Narratives are suited to elaborating the web of relations that make up individual histories of reading and writing. Gender and class can be viewed through the nuances of practices that are felt as well as cognitively known. Girls can be portrayed as complex subjects who assert their agencies, even as their lives are shaped within relationships of material goods, affective ties with others, and practices of schooling. (p. 52)

For both boys and girls, gender creates particular role options and ways of being; children explore these various roles, sometimes assuming nontraditional roles as with Alicia's sister, and at other times reflecting dominant expectations and ways of being.

The challenge for educators is to not only assist children in becoming literate but to help them see themselves as people who use literacy to achieve their personal goals. Identity work is ongoing for Alicia and Jasmine as they encounter productive and potentially limiting experiences with literacy in school. Their stories offer insights into the complexities of identity construction and offer complex and multifaceted accounts that challenge simple explanations. Their stories attest to the fluidity of identity construction and the existence of multiple and potentially contradictory ways of being that provide educators with opportunities for helping children to assume identity positionings that value what they bring and present opportunities for growth. Gender is a part of this process.

Chapter 5

Degrees of Reading Success and Failure: Peter and Bradford

Ms. Holt spoke about her son Bradford's difficulty with reading when he was in my first-grade class: "Well, I figure once he learns how to read then. . . but he doesn't, he don't know how to read so, I don't know. But his brother helps him a lot so that, you know, I guess but that he can read some things." I spoke with her again when Bradford was in fifth grade:

Author: Do you think there is any particular reason why he doesn't like to read as much or why he doesn't like to read more?
Ms. Holt: 'Cause he can't.
Author: Has that gotten better though?
Ms. Holt: Oh, he's better but you know I guess, he can but he gets frustrated and you know when you want to do something and you can't do it and you get frustrated.

Over time Ms. Holt's frustration has increased as she watched her son continue to struggle with reading. In schools across the country many children become accomplished readers. However, many other students, particularly in urban schools, struggle with learning to read. In this chapter, I explore some of the dimensions that define success and failure with reading.

Themes of success and failure occur and reoccur throughout the data collected for this study. Children and parents often describe themselves and their children in terms of their perceived reading abilities; different children positioned themselves very differently and their parents positioned the children differently; these positionings reflect their figured worlds and the criteria that people accept as indicators of reading success. In this chapter, I ground my analysis in the work of Pierre Bourdieu (1986) and present the construct of "reading capital." I then present two case studies that have helped me understand the ways my former students are positioned in terms of their success or failure with reading. I begin by exploring some of the dimensions of reading that are valued or dismissed as children are deemed successful or unsuccessful with reading.

READING CAPITAL: DEFINING READING SUCCESS AND FAILURE

What is it that counts when students are described as being successful or unsuccessful with reading? Current political rhetoric identifies five essential components of reading: phonemic awareness, phonics, fluency, vocabulary, and comprehension (National Reading Panel, 2000). However, the case studies that I present in this chapter suggest that there are other dimensions of reading that are often ignored in schools and by official policy makers. These dimensions relate only marginally to the officially sanctioned components of reading listed above. They draw our attention to the ways in which the experience of learning to read at school is situated within powerful social, cultural, and economic contexts. However, these social, cultural, and economic factors are often ignored while educators and policy makers fixate on methods and materials for teaching reading.

As Gee (1996) explains, middle-class children have a distinct advantage in schools. While learning the dominant discourses of schooling requires extending existing discourses for all children, middle-class children have had constant opportunities to acquire ways of being and thinking that are highly similar to the discourses they encounter in school. Children from poor and racially diverse backgrounds often do not share this advantage and are required to "learn" these school-based discourses when they arrive at school. According to Gee, learning involves gaining conscious knowledge involving explanation and analysis, a process that requires both time and committed effort. Thus participating in the game of schooling and becoming a reader may involve different processes for different children and these processes are enacted on social fields that privilege some and handicap others.

In this chapter, I use Bourdieu's (1986) construct of capital to identify and explore the ways my former students are positioned as successful or unsuccessful readers. While this research cannot claim that these additional dimensions of reading cause a child to be successful or unsuccessful with reading, the case studies presented suggest that officially sanctioned notions of reading coexist alongside the additional dimensions of reading in relationships that may be reciprocally influential.

Critical theorists have used the construct of capital to explore the ways in which particular groups of people and individuals are favored within particular social and economic contexts (Bourdieu, 1986; Luke, 1996).

As Pierre Bourdieu explains, the construct of capital makes it "possible to explain the unequal scholastic achievement of children originating from different social classes" by relating academic success to the ways resources are dispersed in society (p. 243). Recognition of the different amounts of capital that children possess challenges commonsense views that attribute academic success and failure to natural ability or effort. Thus the concept of capital identifies factors beyond personal failure or inferiority as the reasons for a person's success or failure within educational, social, and economic fields. While the construct of capital is often critiqued as being overly deterministic, in this chapter I use the construct of capital not to predict the future success of children, but rather, to identify aspects of reading that can privilege children within the context of school.

Bourdieu (1986) describes three forms of capital: economic capital, social capital, and cultural capital. Distinctions among these forms of capital are revealing when applied to reading. Bourdieu describes *economic capital* as including possessions that are directly convertible into money. *Economic reading capital* involves possessions that are convertible into reading success. Attaining these possessions requires an investment of money into objects or experiences that are believed by the purchaser to help students learn to read. Items such as computers, electronic educational toys, significant numbers of quality books, and costly home reading programs (e.g., Hooked on Phonics) all represent monetary investments in reading that are often believed to contribute to a child's success with reading.

Bourdieu (1986) uses the term *social capital* to refer to connections and group memberships that advantage people within social contexts. "Social reading capital" entails being able to recognize, access, and utilize social relationships to support oneself as a reader. These social relationships include relationships with family members, teachers, and peers, as well as the social networks that exist between families and school personnel that support children as readers. Social networks that provide access to social, economic, and political institutions are particularly rich examples of social reading capital.

As Bourdieu (1986) explains, *cultural capital* exists in three states: embodied capital, objectified capital, and institutionalized capital. *Embodied cultural capital* refers to mannerisms and social practices that favor people within particular contexts. In the reading classroom, students whose words, mannerisms, and gestures fulfill school ideals can be described as possessing *embodied reading capital*. These are the children who read the "right" books, participate in reading in ways that are acceptable at school (i.e., reading as a solitary activity accompanied by workbook exercises and skill practice), and follow school norms for reading behavior (i.e., sitting at a desk, reading silently, decoding words). In addition, these children say the right things about reading (i.e., "I love to read."); they talk about their favorite books, and verbalize the importance of learning to read. These students exhibit an allegiance to school-sanctioned reading norms through their display of embodied reading capital.

Objectified cultural capital refers to services and products that a person creates. *Objectified reading capital* includes student writing, classwork, completed homework, and oral reading that meet school norms for performance. As Bourdieu (1986) explains, objectified capital only has value when it reflects the embodied capital that is officially recognized. In other words, the products and services produced by students must reflect the cultural norms instantiated via embodied capital in order to have value. A piece of writing that is written using African American speech patterns, for example, might not have the objectified capital of a piece of writing that incorporates the conventions of standard English.

The third type of cultural capital described by Bourdieu (1986) is *institutionalized capital.* Institutionalized capital refers to qualifications, certifications, and credentials that are recognized within the larger community. The recent barrage of state testing programs across the United States has created a new form of *institutionalized reading capital*; passing the fourth-grade English Language Arts Test is an institutionally recognized accomplishment. In addition, report card grades, Stanford Nine test scores, and attaining institutionally sanctioned proficiency benchmarks also convey institutionalized reading capital.

PETER AND BRADFORD

Peter and Bradford are very different in terms of their officially recognized success or failure with reading, yet they share a remarkable degree of similarity. Both are African American young men; Peter is in a regular fifth-grade classroom while Bradford is in a self-contained, fifth-grade special education classroom. Both students are the children of single mothers and both have families who support them with reading and writing in a variety of ways. When I assessed the boys in fourth and fifth grade, both exhibited some difficulty with reading texts at their grade level. Both boys have siblings who are very different from them in terms of their school reading success. While Bradford struggles with reading, he has an older brother who has done extremely well. Peter was identified by his teachers as being a remarkable reader while his younger brother is experiencing some difficulties with reading at school. In fifth grade, Peter and Bradford were attending different schools.

Peter and His Family

I was nervous when I returned to visit with the families of my former students. We had little contact over the past 3 years and I was returning to ask them more questions about reading. When I got out of the car, Ms. Horner was standing on the porch with a small baby. She greeted me warmly as always and my nervousness evaporated. We went inside and Ms. Horner showed me pictures of Peter and his younger brother. Ms. Horner was very proud of her new apartment, which was larger than her old one and nicely furnished. The neighborhood was nicer too, with large green lawns where the boys could play. She was absolutely glowing with pride in her new baby and the new home.

Ms. Horner worked for the telephone company and has recently been promoted at her job. She did not graduate from high school, but completed her GED and has been working at the phone company since before I knew her. Ms. Horner's dress, speech, and mannerisms are very compatible with the professional working environment. She reports that the baby's father is now living with them and she seems pleased with this new arrangement.

Peter is the oldest of Ms. Horner's three children. Ever since first grade, Ms. Horner has expressed her pleasure with Peter's school success. When Peter was in first grade, I asked her what it was like being a parent of a child learning to read. She responded: "It's amazing because though he's learning to read, he's doing a lot on his own. So, he does come to me, and you know ask me for help and everything, but I think he makes himself really proud, because he remembers. . . . He tries to do things on his own."

Her enthusiasm continues now that Peter is in fifth grade. "He's been doing great. He really has. Peter—his lowest grade [on his report card] is a B+." At another point in the interviews she remarked, "Every year I get the same comments [from his teachers] what a pleasure he is, how helpful he is, [and] how intelligent he is." Peter agrees; he views himself as a good reader:

Author: Do you think you're a good reader?
Peter: Yes.
Author: How do you know?
Peter: Because I don't usually need help on words and I'm a great speller.
Author: Are you?
Peter: Uh-huh.
Author: How do you know you're a great speller?
Peter: I get hundreds on my spelling tests.

While Peter's reading had many strengths, I was surprised to discover that the two assessments I completed when I interviewed Peter prior to and during his fifth-grade year indicated that Peter had some rather serious difficulties with reading comprehension, although his reading accuracy rates were very high. On my first visit, I used the Developmental Reading Assessment (Beaver, 1997) to determine the level of text that he could read with both accuracy and comprehension. He read 99% of the words correctly in the Level 44 text, Danger in the Deep (Grade 4). His reading was well phrased. He corrected one out of the three errors he made in the text. Both of the uncorrected errors did not make sense in the context of the story. When asked to retell what he had read, Peter displayed a very limited understanding of what he had read. While the characters in the story were preparing to dive for lobster, Peter reported that they had been climbing a mountain and were trying to get back down.

When I visited Peter during January of fifth grade, I used parts of the Shanker/Ekwall Informal Reading Inventory, which includes a graded word list, reading passages, and comprehension questions. While he successfully read the words from the seventh-grade passage, comprehension was a problem; he had difficulty answering comprehension questions.

Bradford and His Family

Bradford and his older brother were in the front yard when I pulled up in my car. Bradford ran ahead of me into the house. By the time I had walked up the driveway, Ms. Holt was at the door greeting me. I was welcomed into a small room that was furnished with only an old worn sofa and chair. Bradford had celebrated his birthday with a sleepover the night before and the last of the guests were just leaving. Bradford is the youngest of seven children; most of Bradford's siblings are in high school and beyond.

The year Bradford was in my class, Ms. Holt had just completed her degree in food service; she was very excited about her new occupation. When I returned to interview her 3 years later, she was on disability recovering from major surgery on her back. Her doctor had informed her that because of her condition she would no longer be able to work in food service. She recreated her conversation with her doctor: "'You can't bend no more so you'll have to find a new profession.' [the doctor said it] just as easy if it's just you and me talking. 'You gonna have to change your profession now,' like [it's nothing]. . . I didn't go to school for a long time just to give up it all. . . I don't know what I'll do now." Ms. Holt is an expressive storyteller; her rolling laugh and engaging stories always make my conversations with her informative and moving. Her deft use of language and rich expressions to capture the nuances of her life make her a valuable and greatly appreciated informant.

When Bradford was in first grade, Ms. Holt reported that he was having difficulty learning to read. By fifth grade, Ms. Holt still had concerns about Bradford's reading. Despite these continuing difficulties, Ms. Holt remained encouraged. Bradford had been retained twice in school. He had been in a self-contained special education class for the past year and at the end of third grade his teachers had spoken to Ms. Holt about mainstreaming him for fifth grade. Ms. Bradford was very excited about this possibility:

> They're going to mainstream him this year 'cause that's what we've been working for from the beginning to get him ready to be mainstreamed and. . . everything [is better] you know his behavior has changed, you know his attitude. I don't know if he was too young to understand what was really going on or [if] he wasn't mature enough to know exactly what was what, but you know I guess as he matured a little bit things have gotten better. I'm very pleased.

However, when I returned for the second interview, Ms. Holt reported that Bradford was never mainstreamed.

> Well see, I was a little disappointed when they, 'cause they kept telling him that they were going to mainstream him. And then his teachers didn't go through the procedures they should have went through to [have him] be mainstreamed. They didn't do [it] 'cause, all last year we were talking mainstreaming him because he was doing much better, he was. His attitude was better, everything was much better. . . and then when I talked to her [last year's teacher] after the meeting [this year] she act like she didn't even [remember]. You know and I was very, very disappointed in that. Very disappointed and Bradford was too.

While Bradford did not identify himself as an unsuccessful reader, his answers to questions often conveyed his frustration with reading. To him learning to read encompassed a series of tasks to be completed. The tone of his voice expressed a sense of futility.

Author: Is there anything that teachers do to help you learn to read?
Bradford: (*pause*) They give me spelling words.
Author: Mmm-hmm.
Bradford: Then I get a book and I have to write a book report about it.

Author: (*laughs*) Yeah? Anything else they do?
Bradford: Nope.

The assessments I did with Bradford confirm that, according to school expectations, he is a struggling reader. Yet despite the many difficulties he has with reading, Bradford possesses some remarkable strengths. During the summer prior to Grade 4, Bradford read a Level 18 (beginning of second grade) text from the Developmental Reading Assessment. The text was beyond Bradford's instructional reading level; he read it with only a 86% accuracy rate. The miscues that Bradford made generally shared some degree of graphophonic similarity with the target word; he read "waked" for "walked," "away" for "always," and "look" for "looking." Many of the miscues that Bradford made clearly disrupted meaning and Bradford rarely reread to self-correct his reading. Totally nonsensical stretches of text were not reread or corrected. As Bradford read through this story, he made more and more miscues as he went. By the end he was frustrated, and I made the decision not to have him read any more selections that day. I was pleasantly surprised, however, when I asked Bradford to retell the story. Despite his awkward and flawed reading, Bradford was able to provide me with a remarkably good retelling of what he had read.

This same phenomenon occurred when I again heard Bradford read 9 months later. I started by having Bradford read the same Level 18 text. This time Bradford read the selection at 90% accuracy, which put the text just barely within his instructional reading range. Bradford was able to monitor and correct more of his miscues by making sure that what he read made sense. However, it was still a struggle for Bradford to attend to both graphophonic cues and making sense. This divided attention may be the reason that Bradford misread several simple words (i.e., reading "there" for "then," "they" for "she," "the" for "to"). Again Bradford's comprehension was remarkably good. At my request Bradford attempted the Level 20 (second grade) text; Bradford was obviously struggling and we stopped after the first two paragraphs.

PETER, BRADFORD, AND READING CAPITAL

Despite the similarities that Peter and Bradford share, there are many differences in their lives and their experiences with reading. Both exhibit some difficulties with reading. While the National Reading Panel (2000) may be content with analyzing reading in terms of phonemic awareness, phonics, fluency, vocabulary, and comprehension, a closer analysis of Peter and Bradford as readers reveals dimensions of reading beyond decoding and comprehension. These additional dimensions of reading involve social and contextual aspects of reading: how reading and learning to read are situated within economic, social, and cultural contexts. In the following sections, I use data from both the original study (Grade 1) and the current study (Grades 4 and 5) to explore the forms of reading capital that Peter and Bradford exhibit.

Economic Reading Capital

Economic reading capital includes those possessions that require an investment of money and are assumed to contribute to a person's success with reading. Neither Peter's nor Bradford's families owns possessions of exceptional monetary value. While Ms. Horner's long-term job and recent promotion have resulted in economic gains for the family, Ms. Holt is currently relying on disability. The prospect of not being able to return to her previous job has dealt a blow to the family income.

In terms of reading, both families have some possessions that support children as readers and have some monetary value. For example, when Peter was in first grade, his mother reported that he had "close to 100" books. In fifth grade Peter connected the possession of these books to his being a good reader.

Author: How do you know you're a good reader?
Peter: Because I always read to my mom and my brother. We have a lot
   of books at home.

Bradford has many fewer books at home than Peter. However, this does not indicate that his family does not value reading or that they are not willing to invest financial resources into supporting Bradford as a reader. His mother, like several of the mothers in the study, reports purchasing educational toys to help Bradford learn to read. When I asked Ms. Holt about Bradford's attitude toward reading in fifth grade, she responded: "You know, he does it [he reads] because he has to. He doesn't, like you [won't] see him pick up a book. Like he's got the little [toy] laptop I bought him a couple years ago to help him with his reading so he'll pull that out rather than a book. "

Economic reading capital refers to the investment of economic resources into commodities that have the perceived potential to contribute to a person's success with reading. In his book *iShop, You Shop* (2001), Patrick Shannon examines how reading has become commodified and sold to teachers and parents. As the cases of Peter and Bradford demonstrate, the commodification of reading can assume various forms. Peter's mother has invested significant amounts of money into purchasing books for Peter. Bradford's mother has purchased an educational electronic toy that has been widely advertised as being helpful to children learning to read. This "laptop" provides children with practice with particular letters, letter sounds, and sight words. These purchases both entail significant amounts of economic reading capital. However, their use provides each of these boys with very different reading experiences that differentially translate into reading in the classroom. While reading books supports dominant discourses that define appropriate home reading experiences, electronic toys are generally not among the home reading activities that teachers recommend to families. Electronic toys that teach letters, sounds, and words have a limited application to school reading tasks and relate only minimally to the strategies children need to read connected text. While Peter's practice with reading books may support him with school reading tasks, Bradford's electronic drills with letters and words may be helpful but limited in terms of its effect on his reading progress, especially at this point when he is already familiar with the letters and the sounds that they make. By fourth and fifth grades the tests that children take involve extensive reading and writing activities that bear little resemblance to the phonetic drills.

Social Reading Capital

Social reading capital refers to connections and group memberships that support success with reading. Social reading capital involves being able to recognize, access, and utilize social relationships as means to support oneself as a reader. Peter has always described reading as a social activity. While my other first-grade students typically listed family members when I asked them who helped them learn to read, Peter mentioned his friends at day care.

Peter: Sometimes when I have homework, when I don't know what the word says, they help me out.
Author: Are they grown-up friends or kid friends?
Peter: Kid friends.

The theme of helping others with reading reoccurs across many of Peter's interview and is illustrated in Figure 5.1. It is also evident in his description of sharing books with his best friend, Louis:

Peter: He [Louis] has collections of *Goosebumps* books and he gives me some.

Figure 5.1. Peter as a Social Reader

Grade 1

Author: How do you know Leshanda is a good reader?
Peter: Because sometimes I sit with her and help her read so then she be reading the whole book.
Author: Is there anything that you would like to do better when you read?
Peter: Yes.
Author: What's that?
Peter: Help somebody.
Author: How would you help somebody?
Peter: Help them with the words.

Grade 4

Author: What's the best thing you've ever done in school any year?
Peter: (*Long pause*) Help my friends. They are really important to me.
Author: Are they? Do you have lots of friends?
Peter: Yes.
Author: Are there any projects that you and your friends really liked that were really super?
Peter: Well sometimes we have to do like a book report or something and we gather up together and we do a, we do a report on a book that we all agree on.

Author: So, you like *Goosebumps* too?
Peter: Uh-huh!

For Peter, reading connects him with his peer group. As I got ready to leave one interview, Peter said he had something for me and ran upstairs bringing back the *Goosebumps* book that he had just finished reading; he suggested that I read it. I declined saying that he should trade it with a friend for a new one to read; he agreed. These social experiences around reading, along with supportive interactions that occur with his mother and his teachers, have provided Peter with an extensive social network that supported him as he learned to read.

Bradford describes supportive reading relationships with his mother, and both Bradford and his mother explain how his older brothers and sisters have supported him. Unlike Peter, Bradford does not view school reading as a pleasurable social activity. During first grade I wrote in my field notes that Bradford is "sometimes nervous when put on the spot with reading [aloud to me]." By fifth grade, Bradford spoke about this discomfort. He explained that it bothered him when other people were around when he's reading, "'cause they distract me." When I asked Bradford what things make learning to read hard, he responded, "When I get nervous . . . sometimes I get scared when I don't know how to pronounce every

word." Because of his nervousness with reading, Bradford reported that
the teacher allowed him to sit by himself in the back of the room.

Despite these discouraging reports, when Bradford was in first grade
I inadvertently captured him reading enthusiastically and competently
on tape with a friend. Bradford and Jerome, another struggling reader,
were reading a story that I had introduced to them during our guided
reading group. I left the tape recorder running while I went to answer
the telephone. It was weeks later while transcribing that tape that I heard
the remarkable and lengthy interaction that occurred between Bradford
and Jerome as they collaborated to read the text. Unfortunately, instances
such as these were rare.

One of Bradford's older brothers, who is described by his mother as
being a wonderful reader and is now in college, struggled with stuttering
when he was in school. Bradford describes how his brother helps him: "He
told me, uh, stop talking, stop talking in the classroom and read. And take
it slow. . . They used to call him stutter Mario." Interestingly, his brother's
advice about reading involves not talking. This emphasis on eliminating the
social brings to mind Ms. Holt's words from our first interview when she
explained that unlike some of her children she could not see herself sitting
around reading "thick old, big old books." She explains that Bradford is
like her in that way: "I guess he can't sit still that long." In contrast to Peter
who views reading as a socially interactive experience, Bradford, and his
mother, tend to view reading as solitary and sedentary.

Social reading capital also involves the social relationships that exist
between families and school personnel that support children as readers.
These relationships can also contribute to students being successful or
unsuccessful with reading. Peter has consistently developed positive
relationships with his teachers and these relationships have fostered good
relationships between his mother and his teachers. Ms. Horner explains
that teachers consistently view Peter as helpful and intelligent. Thus Ms.
Horner's relationship with the school has been positive.

Bradford's school history has been very different. Relationships with
teachers and school officials have often been strained by a lack of communication, lack of school follow-through, Bradford's sometimes difficult behavior, and Bradford's difficulties with learning to read. In addition to the conflict surrounding whether Bradford should be placed in a
mainstream classroom, Ms. Holt also described the difficulties she faced
when he was initially placed in special education. She describes how
"terrible" it was as she "battled" with the board of education:

> I had a lawyer and a advocate. . . . She [the teacher] just, she wasn't
> pleased. I was not pleased and I'm struggling too hard to get Bradford

[going] and then he got to the point where he didn't want to do anything. And I saw myself losing him. And I didn't want to do that. You know, I didn't want to lose him like that. So they told me they couldn't do this and they wanted to put him in a 6-1-1 [six students, one teacher, and one paraprofessional; a severely restrictive special education placement]. Oh, no, no, no. Nope, nope, nope, nope. That's how I started, nope. [The district representatives asked me,] "What do you think?" [I answered,] "Nope. I don't care what you think." And that's how I started [the conversation].

Ms. Holt explained her decision, "It's gonna make his, lower his self-esteem and you know that's [a] kid that's 11 or 12 [years old]." Ms. Holt, with the help of the lawyer and advocate, was successful in having Bradford placed in the 12-1-1 classroom.

Finally, Bradford and his mother have also faced conflicts with some of his teachers. Ms. Holt describes a conversation she had with one of his teachers the year before. "Like I told Miss Dobson. . . and I said you can't treat all the kids the same you just [can't] . . .and he [Bradford] gets offended with the military style. . . And I told her she just gotta kinda gently ease up on that tactic." Ms. Holt reports that this conversation resulted in the teacher "easing up" on Bradford. However, at a later interview, Ms. Holt explains that Miss Dobson continues to "harass" Bradford at school even though he is no longer in her class. Ms. Holt blames Miss Dobson for failing to have Bradford placed in the mainstream classroom.

When dealing with teachers and the school on her own, she was often dismissed and her interests were ignored. While Ms. Holt's interest in her son is clearly evident, we must ask how her status as a poor, single, and Black parent, along with her physical and linguistic characteristics, are interpreted by school personnel. Do her accomplished use of African American speech patterns, her booming voice, and her creative expressions work against her in the Standard English world of school? Do the loud colors she wears and her stylish hair gain more attention than her message?

Cultural Reading Capital

As I explained earlier, cultural reading capital exists in three states: embodied reading capital, objectified reading capital, and institutionalized reading capital.

Embodied Reading Capital. Embodied reading capital refers to mannerisms and social practices that contribute to students being defined as successful readers. Embodied reading capital includes words, mannerisms, and gestures that reflect school ideals about reading.

Both Peter and Bradford access official discourses about reading. They both talk about going to college, the importance of paying attention, and moving on to higher grades (see Figure 5.2). However, Peter's language often moves beyond these verbiages to capture particulars about the relationship between reading and eventual success. He talks about teachers helping students, students reading "a lot" and reading "often," and the relationship between reading and employment. The specificity of Peter's language displays an acceptance of official understandings about the importance of reading that reflects the embodied reading capital Peter possesses. The ways Peter talks about reading are clearly rooted in official discourses that schools and teachers value.

In contrast, while Bradford voices some school-sanctioned discourses about reading, he refers to only institutional manifestations of reading (i.e., going to college, moving up to other grades) while only making vague references to personal purposes for reading (i.e., "learning" and "getting smart"). Peter is much more adept at voicing these discourses; he seems comfortable subscribing to them and expresses faith in their potential. Perhaps Bradford's struggles with learning to read in school have discouraged him, leading to a disillusionment with dominant discourses about reading. However, his frustration alone may not explain his dubious voicing of school-sanctioned discourses about reading.

Bradford is the youngest of seven children. Although his mother reports that some of his brothers and sisters are avid readers and one brother is now attending college, Bradford's older siblings have faced many challenges that have not been solved by their ability to read. For example, when Bradford was in first grade, his mother spoke of Bradford's older brother who was in special education classes at a district high school. This brother was on the honor roll during the spring of his senior year of high school and was suddenly told that he would not graduate. Although Ms. Holt spoke with school officials several times, she was never able to obtain a clear explanation for why her son's graduation was denied. Meanwhile her son became so "disgusted" with the situation that he refused to even consider the possibility of returning to school. Even Ms. Holt's children who were successful readers have faced challenges beyond high school. Her eldest son was killed in a DWI accident. Her daughter graduated from high school but has not continued her education nor attained more than a minimum wage job. Another son dropped out of high school and is pursuing a GED. These and other similarly frustrating experiences with schools have contributed to the erosion of Ms. Holt's confidence in the power of schools to help her chil-

Figure 5.2. Peter's and Bradford's Embodied Reading Capital

Peter—Grade 1

"You can learn much [by reading]."

"You can get to higher grades [by reading]. . . and you could go to college"

"The teachers help them [the students] and they have to pay attention."

Peter—Grade 5

"Sometimes you have to do important things and you might not know how unless you read the instructions."

"You'll never get a job if you can't read because they take people that are smart and read a lot."

"[Children have trouble learning to read because] they don't try hard enough or they don't read very often."

Bradford—Grade 1

"[Reading is important because] you get smart. . . you go to college."

Bradford—Grade 4

"[If you can't read] you won't go to other grades. . . [You] won't learn."

"[It's hard for kids to learn when] they don't pay attention when the teacher's telling you stuff."

---

dren. When Bradford was in first grade, Ms. Holt spoke about her frustration with the educational system:

> I'm so disgusted now with my son [who had just been pushed out of high school] I could just—when something like that happen I could tell them oh you don't have to go to school 'cause this gonna happen to you when you get to 12th and you never knew a thing. I could just make them be discouraged instead of [saying] no, "You're going to work through it."

By the time Bradford was in fifth grade, Ms. Holt's fears for Bradford focused on his future. School was presented as an obstacle that Bradford must endure.

> [I worry] that he gets disgusted and don't want to finish [school]. . . . That does bother me if that happens but I'm gonna stick behind him,

for I'm going to, I'll TRY not to let that happen. See what I'm saying, 'cause I'm going to encourage him, you know. If I tell him, "A couple more years, whatever happens just two more years" and then try to get [him] into ROTC, that's the way. They got good things.

Although Ms. Holt maintained that school was important and stated that she would "stick behind him," school was something to get through rather than a place of possibilities for Bradford.

When we examine the experiences of this family, it is easy to begin to understand why Bradford may have adopted a dubious attitude toward the official discourses about reading. With the exception of his brother who has started college, reading has not led to success for his siblings. Both Bradford and his mother emphasize reading as a means to maneuver school (i.e., move on to the next grade, get into college) rather than as a personal accomplishment or social experience. Their emphasis is on surviving the educational system rather than personal accomplishment.

This does not imply that Bradford's family members do not care about reading, do not enjoy reading, or do not feel strongly that reading is important. Ever since Bradford was in first grade, Ms. Holt has had very strong views on the importance of reading: "I think it is very important that Bradford learns how to read because of his future. If he can't read he's not going to go anyplace in this world."

While Ms. Holt explained in early interviews that she "never liked to read," she now says "I enjoy reading." She explained that her daughter started to bring home books by Donald Goines (Goines, 2000; Goines & Locke, 1999) and she surprised herself with her reading:

> [In high school] we read. . . a book called *Black Girl*. And then my daughter she got it and once she came home with a couple of them. *Red Men*, he [Donald Goines] has a whole bunch of them. And [when] she gets them out we be reading them and I realize that book's all gone [*Ms. Holt laughs*]. I read the whole book. Oh God! Knowledge! [*We both laugh.*]

Ms. Holt now enjoys reading; yet Bradford struggles with reading at school.

In contrast, Peter has found school to be a place that values him and his efforts with reading. Without the experiences of older siblings to confirm or contradict the possibilities presented by school, Ms. Horner sees Peter as poised for success in school:

What can I not say about Peter? Peter, I am so proud of him. He makes me so happy. He really does. In school he's a model citizen. They have this thing called "Model Citizen." And he's a Model Citizen every year. He's just—he's truly wonderful. He tutors in school. . . . The students that work well, they have like independent time to themselves and everything.

Thus Ms. Horner's and Peter's talk about reading reflect school-sanctioned norms about reading and an allegiance to school-sanctioned expectations. Peter exhibits large amounts of embodied reading capital. He says the right things, behaves in the right ways, and has adopted official discourses that suggest that reading in school will contribute to more than surviving school, and will contribute to personal and professional success.

Bradford finds himself in a much more complicated situation. His own experiences as a frustrated reader along with the mixed experiences of his family members make him less able dogmatically to accept official discourses about reading, and he is understandably cautious about ascribing to official discourses about reading. By failing to voice these discourses, by not talking about reading in the right ways, and by not behaving in accordance with school-sanctioned expectations around reading, Bradford puts himself at risk by not displaying large amounts of embodied reading capital despite the fact that the school system itself has contributed to Bradford's hesitancy to ascribe to these discourses.

Objectified Reading Capital. Objectified reading capital refers to reading services and products that a person creates and that are valued within schools. Objectified reading capital includes student writing, classwork, teacher-created tests, and oral reading that meet school norms for performance. Both Peter and Bradford exhibit objectified reading capital. For example, both students have done well on tests in their classrooms:

Peter: Right now I'm in the bush leagues because my teacher said that. She was passing back the papers, and then she said on the other test everybody else got in the minor leagues and . . . only one person got a hundred and then when I came to pick up my test, I got one hundred and that's what people said, "I hate him. He always get hundreds."

Author: What did you have to do in social studies that you liked?
Bradford: A one hundred.

Author: A hundred what?
Bradford: A hundred in social studies.
Author: Wow, on, on, what's it on?
Bradford: Black history.

As Peter's comment suggests, he is consistent in attaining high grades. Bradford's high score on his Black history test is clearly a momentous event and both Bradford and his mother mention this achievement; unfortunately Bradford is less consistent in obtaining high test scores.

In addition to tests, the quality of a student's work can also demonstrate objectified reading capital. The following writing samples solicited during the research process provide insight into the tendency of each of these students to produce pieces of writing that fulfill classroom expectations. Each student was asked to write a story about school.

Peter's Story: The bad music Note

One day, I was at a ~~chorus~~ choir ~~real~~ rehearsal, one of the first times. ~~W~~ When we were practicing a song I slipped a note out my mouth which made everyone laugh. On my way back, one of my friends copied what I did and we started to giggle through class.

On the next day, we were at lunch talking about how choir and how cool it was. All of a sudden my friends brought up what started the laughter. People laughed hard but it stopped when the principal came in.

Bradford's Story

When ~~the~~ my class be talking out ~~low~~ [loud] of tran [turn]. When we be mak~~e~~ing fun of the kid. When I get mad I will have to go outside of the class.

Clearly vast differences are apparent between Peter's and Bradford's writing. Peter's story follows a conventional story schema in which there is a situation (the "slipped note"), events (the repeated bouts of laughter), a problem (the principal), and a resolution (the laughing stopped). In contrast, Bradford's story is about misbehavior in class. His first two sentences present a situation, but the third sentence does not clearly relate to the others. The reader remains unclear as to why Bradford was upset and why he had to leave the class. Problems are introduced but they are left unresolved. Bradford's message remains unclear and his story does not fit the conventions for storytelling in school. Peter is able to convey his story in ways that are valued and expected in classrooms. Bradford clearly has a compelling and poignant story to tell, yet he does not present it in a school-sanctioned form. While Peter's story brings with it a degree of objectified capital, Bradford's does not. Furthermore, Peter's story captures him playing a socially valued role among his peers, Bradford's story is about isolation from his peers.

Yet Bradford fulfills other school-valued norms. For example, both Bradford's teacher and mother share enthusiasm for his consistency in getting his homework done. As Ms. Holt reports, "He did real good homework. They [the teachers] were very impressed with his homework this year. I think he only missed one." According to his mother, Peter is also very good about completing homework, although she does mention that "each year he has, he has a moment where he um where he's not handing in his homework."

Both boys can produce products (high test scores, homework assignments) that carry objectified reading capital. While Bradford appears to be more consistent with completing his homework, Peter consistently obtains high scores on tests and is able to produce writing that approximates the expectations of the classroom and the larger society. Interestingly, Peter's consistently high test scores and writing ability appear to carry more objectified capital than Bradford's success in completing his homework.

Institutionalized Reading Capital. Institutionalized reading capital refers to qualifications, certifications, and credentials related to reading that are recognized within the larger community. Report card grades, state test scores, and other standardized tests are evidence of institutionalized reading capital. Peter passed the state fourth-grade ELA test; Bradford did not.

While Peter's mother reports that his lowest report card grade was a B+, Bradford's mother expresses great concern and confusion about her son's report card grades, as I noted in Chapter 2. Although Bradford gets As and Bs on his classwork, his report card grades are low.

> When I get his report card, it has all Ds on it. . . . I'm not going to deal with [Bradford's] attitude; it's much better. But I'm talking about academically, he [the teacher] said he [Bradford] was doing good in math and reading doing much better, but he was getting all Ds on his report card. I said, "I can't really understand. I really can't understand that. If he's doing so well why don't you show me this on his report card?"

Again, although Bradford does at times demonstrate degrees of institutionalized reading capital, he does not exhibit them consistently.

THE INTERSECTION OF RACE WITH READING CAPITAL

The fact that both Peter and Bradford are African American, yet both are defined very differently in terms of their success or failure with reading, may seem to suggest that race is not a critical factor in reading success or failure. However, a closer look at the data reveals a very different interpretation. When I asked both of their mothers whether schools discriminate against certain groups of people, Peter's and Bradford's mothers responded differently. Ms. Horner explained:

> Um, speaking from my own experience I haven't noticed something like that. . . I just feel that city schools are geared to um more [toward the] African American community. So I think, I do believe that they um, the schools try to come up with programs um to help the kids.

Ms. Holt cites the different ways different schools are treated in the media as evidence of the inequities among schools:

> It's like, I think it was last week on the news....They had these two schools on the east and the west [side of the city] . . . and they going to have a competition . . . and the school's going to get a lot of competence [compensation], a thousand dollars.... Why didn't they come into the city and get North High? Johnson [High]? There weren't any city schools. And they kept it, they could have used one of those for example. So why did they use just suburban schools? You know, I didn't think that was really fair *(laughs).*

While she does not explicitly reference race, Ms. Holt described how suburban schools compare to city schools. She describes suburban schools as being "brand new" and says that when she attended suburban schools her "friends graduated" from high school, unlike her friends in the city. She also talks about the lack of money in urban schools and programs constantly being cut. In contrast, Ms. Horner identifies benefits in attending city schools; she explains that city schools focus more on African American students.

Race also enters the interviews in a way that suggests possibilities for instruction. While neither Peter nor his mother mentioned race when asked about reading, both Ms. Holt and Bradford described successes in reading or school that involve texts connected to their African American heritage. Ms. Holt describes reading books by an African American author, Donald Goines; she describes these books as "street books." Interestingly, Ms. Holt explains that she read her first book by Goines in high school and started reading them again when her daughter recently brought some home. Both Bradford and his mother mentioned Bradford getting a hundred on a social studies test that was focused on Black history.

Although Bradford may have difficulty participating in, accepting, and complying with the official discourses that characterize school reading, texts that portray experiences that are relevant and interesting to him have the potential to help him engage with the established structures of school reading programs. Books that portray people of his own race may to a degree counteract some of the distancing that mediates Bradford's participation in officially defined school reading instruction. Ms. Holt explains, "I tell you what would work with inner city kids, with Black children, let them read about Black people. If they read more about their culture and things that they're doing."

Although they disagree on the success that the district is having in incorporating African American history and culture into instructional programs, both Ms. Horner and Ms. Holt identify race as a factor that affects their child's school experiences. Ms. Holt's words echo proponents of multicultural and Afrocentric programs who advocate using books that reflect the race of the students. They suggest that these texts present remarkable possibilities for students who are disenfranchised from official school reading practices through the inclusion of materials that portray African American experiences and history.

UNRECOGNIZED FAILURES AND SUCCESSES

Peter's Failures

Both Peter and his mother view him as a successful reader. His report card grades and his mother's reports of teacher's comments support this judgment. However, I was very concerned when I assessed Peter's comprehension of what he read. During both assessments, Peter struggled to understand what he read. Peter's case raises a significant question: How can a child with poor comprehension skills be defined by the school, his mother, and himself as a highly competent reader?

When I asked Peter if he needed help with his own reading, he responded, "Yes, with my pace. . . I go, at the moment, too slow." Although he reports that neither his mother nor his teacher shares this self-assessment, he says, "I just think I am not going fast enough." Peter values fast, fluent reading and he is a fast and fluent reader. Too often if children decode print accurately and fluently, they are defined as successful readers. However, Peter's difficulties with making sense of what he reads are perhaps equally as problematic as Bradford's difficulty in reading accurately and fluently; despite Bradford's difficulties with accuracy and fluency, he understands what he reads remarkably well.

Peter's stocks of reading capital obfuscate the very real difficulties he is having with reading. While he easily decodes challenging text, he struggles to discuss what he has read; his vision of good reading involves speed over understanding. While teachers who hear Peter reading fluently in class may assume that he understands what he reads, over time his difficulties with comprehension may become problematic. The school-defined successes that he enjoys may not reflect his true reading ability. Serious concerns are raised by the school's apparent neglect of the difficulties Peter faces with comprehension.

Bradford's Successes

Just as Peter displays some weaknesses that have not been recognized in school, Bradford displays some remarkable abilities. For example, Bradford's ability to comprehend what he reads is not mentioned by either Bradford or his mother. Bradford displays other remarkable strengths that are rarely recognized and not accessed in school. Ms. Holt explains that he has developed a real talent in sports: "He be, him into sports. He like all kinds of sports. Football, now he's into baseball. He be the best at baseball too. He be very good." In addition, Bradford's mom has been very encouraged by Bradford's recent interest in church: "It's [church] changed his whole attitude about everything. He was always helpful but these days [he's] more helpful. He's changed. He always smiles all the time now. He's just a whole different Bradford." She describes church as being a place where Bradford is successful:

> I mean this [church] is the first thing I think he was so good in. You know. I know but look at what he's done now. I can't understand it you know. I mean, (*unclear phrase*) he [a man at church] was telling me all these good qualities in Bradford. Bradford has joined this group. He's joined this group. He's doing this.

Finally, Ms. Holt describes how his teacher noticed Bradford's interest in current events. Ms. Holt reports the teacher's comment, "Ms. Holt,

Bradford knows about these current events." She explains:

> I said [to the teacher] well he just sits there and watches the news. You know nobody tell him, he gets up in the morning, turns it right on to the news channel. . .'cause all my kids sat down and watched the news see what's going on in the world. And to see what's new, what's going on. . . . I wish he would read better cause if he read better he'd read the newspaper like me.

Bradford's teacher did recognize his interest in current events; however, there appeared to be no attempt to use that interest, or any of his other interests, to support him as a reader. Bradford clearly demonstrates strengths and abilities but these remain outside the official boundaries of school.

CONCLUSIONS

This chapter has presented the cases of two students, Peter, who is described by teachers and parents as successful with reading, and Bradford, who is described as not successful. By using Bourdieu's (1986) construct of capital and exploring the presence and absence of different types of reading capital, we begin to reveal various dimensions of reading success in classrooms and identify factors beyond the mechanics of reading that contribute to students' positioning as successful or unsuccessful readers. Reading practices that privilege children include the following:

- Having access to books at home that reflect school ideals of literature and literacy
- Enjoying supportive friends and family relations that involve reading activities
- Benefiting from strong collaborative relationships between children's teachers and parents
- Embodying acceptable attitudes and values related to reading and schooling
- Displaying appropriate behaviors in classroom contexts,
- Creating valued literacy artifacts that reflect school expectations for success, and
- Participating in school activities in ways that lead to meeting school benchmarks, passing tests, and being promoted to the next grade

Engaging in these reading practices involves access to various forms of capital including economic reading capital, social reading capital, and forms of cultural reading capital. Children's success and failure with reading involve the figured worlds of teachers and parents. These figured worlds highlight particular ways of being and particular types of knowing as significant criteria for the success. As Peter's and Bradford's first-grade teacher, I clearly contributed to their official success and failure as readers. I celebrated when Peter read grade-level texts fluently and accurately. I was aware that his comprehension was weak, but assumed that it would improve as he matured. Likewise, I was the teacher who first referred Bradford for special education. I noted the delay in his progress and became frustrated when he did not achieve the progress demonstrated by other children in the class. I failed to recognize his ability to comprehend text and I failed to develop social networks within the classroom that would support Bradford as a reader. Within my figured world as a first-grade teacher, accuracy was a relevant criteria for reading success and it was assumed that comprehension would continue to develop over time.

For Peter and Bradford, success and failure with reading were defined within a school that was considered a failure and was struggling to improve students' reading scores in order to be removed from the state's list of poor-performing schools. Accuracy and decoding were emphasized while comprehension, the ultimate goal of reading, was not; teachers who heard children reading accurately and fluently assumed that comprehension was occurring and turned their attention to children who struggled to decode.

What should I, and other teachers at my school, have done to recognize and develop the many strengths that Bradford brought to the reading classroom? How could we have helped Bradford to become a better reader without positioning him as a failure? How could we have developed his strengths so that he could become a member of the reading communities that exist both in his home and in school? I share Ms. Holt's concerns about Bradford's future:

> Him not succeeding. You know . . . I try to do everything but you know, if he followed my rules he'd be OK, but then he'd go astray and he'd do all kinds of you know. And that's, I got a feeling that, you know, he'll go astray. But if he didn't go to school, he'd go astray. But if he can get to something [that he is successful with].

The challenges of being poor and living in a struggling community are severe. Bradford's school experiences, and particularly his experiences with reading, have provided little that will insulate him from these challenges. Ms. Holt recognizes these challenges, yet also recognizes the possibility that "if he can get to something [that he is successful with],"

Bradford will have an option and an opportunity. However, the set of opportunities offered to Bradford in my classroom involved few opportunities for success. Low reading groups, easier books than the other children were reading, and frustration with writing tasks failed to acknowledge the strengths that Bradford brought. In Peter's case, I was satisfied with accurate decoding.

School-sanctioned notions of reading are accompanied by other dimensions of reading that contribute to identification as either a successful or unsuccessful reader. The adaptation of Bourdieu's (1986) notion of capital has revealed additional dimensions of reading that are often ignored, overlooked, or dismissed:

- What economic investments have parents made into their children's success with reading, and how do those investments converge or conflict with school-sanctioned notions of reading?
- How well have the children mastered school-sanctioned discourses about reading? Do the children play the expected role in terms of their attitude and behaviors around reading?
- What are the social relationships that accompany learning to read, and how do the children position themselves or find themselves positioned within the classroom reading community?
- What is the quality of the social networks that exist between home and school, and how have past school experiences of family members strengthened or weakened these networks of support?
- How are children positioned by their experiences and by their families' experiences to either accept or challenge official discourses about reading? Is it our goal to have children adopt official discourses about reading? Or must we design instructional programs that accommodate alternative ways of being and knowing?
- How do we address the relative valuing and dismissal of various student-created products so that all children's contributions are recognized and developed?
- Finally, can we help children and parents recognize the ways in which school reading success is constructed so that they can make sense of the sometimes contradictory messages they receive from schools?

It is important to realize that reading success in school is not merely based on reading ability. As Bourdieu's (1986) model reveals, reading success involves more than reading. Embodiments associated with being a good reader, social relationships that support reading, and economic investments that support reading are significant. While as teachers we often profess to be concerned only with mechanical aspects of reading, I suggest that we also respond, perhaps unconsciously, to other factors. Children's abilities as readers are enmeshed with particular ways of behaving in classrooms, ways of talking about reading, prior experiences with high-quality texts, and social relationships that support reading. As a system, we can unknowingly, or knowingly, continue to reproduce the established social order by continuing to value particular types of literacy practices and attitudes as the determinants of school success and failure. Conversely, we can recognize that reading success and failure can be defined in multiple ways that sometimes transcend official discourses about reading. In other words, schools and teachers can recognize and value or dismiss and reject the literacy knowledges that children bring to school. All of the children in my class can be viewed as possessing various knowledges and abilities that schools and teachers have the potential to validate and develop.

Bourdieu (1986) applies the concept of capital to adults who are generally in a position of either possessing or not possessing particular forms of capital at a particular point in their lives. I am applying the concept of reading capital in this chapter to children as they are in the process of acquiring forms of capital as they learn to read. Children arrive in my classroom with various types and degrees of capital already in their possession, and teachers are expected to help children acquire additional skills and abilities. All of my students enter with various linguistic and literacy knowledges that they bring from their homes and communities. My job is to acknowledge the abilities they bring while helping them to acquire others. However, teachers, like parents and children, are caught up in figured worlds that identify particular issues and abilities as significant and challenge the significance of others. There is an eternal danger in this. What we attend to might not be enough. If dominant ways of understanding the teaching of reading do not recognize the full range of factors that position children as successful and unsuccessful readers, then Bradford will always be left behind.

Chapter 6

Rereading Conclusions

Marvin and Jermaine, Alicia and Jasmine, and Peter and Bradford all inhabit figured worlds that are constantly being constructed and re-constructed as the children integrate their existing understandings of the worlds with novel experiences. Their figured worlds are not individual creations nor are they created at particular points in time. Their figured worlds share social and historical roots with their family members and peers. Time is a constant and students' figured worlds are never stagnant. In first grade, Jermaine struggled to make friends and fit in with the other children; by fourth grade he was getting into fights. Jasmine was doing well in a first-grade classroom, but her mother worried about her being retained in fifth grade. Alicia, who was always talkative, found that talking in class was becoming a bigger problem in fifth grade.

The case studies in this book have presented the reading experiences of a group of children as they move through elementary school. Their experiences are important. Although we have many research studies that examine children at various points in their lives (Bartlett, 2005; Flores-Gonzalez, 2002; Godley, 2003; Hicks, 2002; Lewis, 2001; Rymes, 2001), we have remarkably few studies that examine children's lives and literacy learning over significant periods of time. While we often blame the learning difficulties of urban children on challenging urban communities or struggling schools, we actually have very little understanding of how environments and experiences converge in the lives of children over time and space. In this longitudinal study, I have used the concept of figured worlds to begin to examine children's literacy experiences as children progressed through elementary school.

In addition to figured worlds (Holland et al., 1998), I have used a range of theoretical constructs—"Discourses" (Gee, 1992, 1996, 1999), theories of identity (McCarthey & Moje, 2002), and theories of capital (Bourdieu, 1986; Luke 1996)—to interpret the words and experiences of the children and their parents. The construct of figured worlds has helped us to understand that children, like all of us, construct understandings of the worlds they inhabit and that these constructions are intimately tied to people and situations they encounter. These figured worlds feature sets of roles and positionings that the children in this study explore; children assume the role of good student one moment and then are sent to the office or yelled at by their teacher the next. They fight at school while aspiring to become police officers, and they read with their friends in the cafeteria but resist the books assigned by the teacher.

Figured worlds are populated by dominant discourses, generally accepted and unexamined ways of understanding the world: Reading is sounding out words, urban parents are negligent, paying attention is the key to learning, and high-stakes testing will address the inequities in our world. While dominant discourses are routinely voiced by participants they are also challenged by participants' stories and their experiences. Children do not actually sound out words when they read, and the lives of the parents in this study challenge negative assumptions about urban parents. Like all of us, the people in this study contradict their own words and behave in ways that challenge the statements they make; their voicing of alternative discourses reminds us that there are many ways of understanding the world and that dominant discourses often fail to account for the complexities of people's lives. Figured worlds are not coherent and stable places; they are rich, complex, and ever changing.

Finally, figured worlds, the discourses that operate within those figured worlds, and the identity positionings that children accept and reject are all in constant interaction with officially sanctioned notions of reading success. Understanding children's successes as readers requires educators to look beyond surface indicators of reading ability and to consider the types of capital related to reading that are valued and celebrated in schools. What are the ways of reading and participating in reading activities that schools value, and what is considered evidence of accomplished reading? As educators, our figured worlds incorporate nuanced understandings about reading success although we may not be aware of the ways reading is enmeshed with attitudes, values, behaviors, and ways of being readers.

This book has presented the first two phases of a very promising model for conducting longitudinal research. By returning to visit children and families at particular intervals over long periods of time, complexities are captured that short-term research snapshots would miss. While this book is not specifically about race, class, gender, discrimination, equity, disability, or access, the stories that weave through its pages reference all of these issues. Children are placed in special education; parents advocate that their children not be pushed through school; significant numbers of children fail their state ELA tests; some parents complain that their children's schools are racist; parents lament the parenting practices of other urban parents; and parents and children describe a lack of respect from teachers. These experiences are not separate from issues of equity and power. This book is about multiple and intertwined complexities that constantly and continuously exist in the lives of children. The longitudinal data presented in this book complicate our understandings by revealing the ways children's lives are deeply contextualized in multiple contexts that are constantly subject to change and how children work to accommodate these changes into their figured worlds as well as to define their own roles within those figured worlds.

HEARING ALTERNATIVE DISCOURSES

For us as educators, this book presents children's and parents' stories that help us think in new ways about the children we encounter. As Bakhtin (1994) explains, words and understandings grounded in the lived experiences of people are devalued within communities of power, and alternative ways of understanding the world are quelled and silenced. Alternative discourses do exist and are expressed—sometimes directly through words and at other times through the actions and experiences of people. While these alternative discourses are often difficult to hear, their very existence offers hope and new possibilities.

As we move through our daily routines, we are caught up with curricular expectations and school policies and it is easy to miss the stories children and their families tell. Explanations are dismissed as excuses, and subtle insights on the part of children and parents go unnoticed. It is important for us to recognize that silence often surrounds the comments and thoughts of students and parents; because educators inhabit positions of relative power in relation to parents and children, they are often reluctant to share their stories. Thoughtful and sensitive attempts on the part of the listener must be made. The language systems controlled by ruling classes, in particular educational institutions, are never adequate for conveying ideas from the margins. Bakhtin explains that dominant ways of understanding the world are historically and culturally constructed and that unofficial ways of knowing are often silenced or censured; "what is unofficial cannot be so fully formulated and expressed" (Bakhtin, 1994, p. 9).

Joanne Devine (1994) describes "muted group theory" that examines the "impact of asymmetrical or uneven power relationships within a society on access to language forms" (p. 222). Rather than viewing literacy learning as a personal achievement or failure, "muted group theory" acknowledges that certain types of language and literacy are privileged over others. Devine reminds us that privileged language forms are created and maintained by particular groups of people and that these privileged language forms articulate and convey the values, beliefs, and attitudes of the groups of people who constructed and control the language. For example, the emotion and social critique that inhabit rap music could not be expressed in standard forms of English; other language and communication forms had to be used. Meanwhile, the socially critical messages that the music presents are often lost when critics focus on the language and word choice. Thus the language of the privileged elite does not serve all groups equally well. Nondominant groups often find themselves with a loss of words or silent when they are required to use the language of the powerful elite to convey their experiences and values. In my own research, as parents encountered contradictions between their own experiences and dominant discourses, their words were often marked with the phrase "I don't know" or a similar hedge suggesting their reluctance to trust their own feelings or a hesitancy to voice dissenting readings based on their own experiences.

As Fine (2003) reports, silence on the part of students is a natural expectation and generally remains unquestioned and unexamined. Many researchers, theoreticians, and practitioners would agree that all students need opportunities to learn to read, write, and speak with a mastery of the dominant literacy practices that will provide them with access to resources and institutions. However, Pam Gilbert (1994) reminds us that "such opportunities need to be accompanied by social understandings of how these practices have become dominant, how their dominance has been maintained, and whose voices and lives have been consequently marginalized or silenced" (p. 125).

One of our roles as educators must be to strive to hear the stories of children and parents. It is only by considering their renditions of their experiences and glimpsing into their figured worlds that we can begin to identify and address the challenges that they face in school and find ways to construct educational experiences that make sense for the children we serve and their families.

Data from longitudinal studies, such as the one described in this book, have the potential to begin to help us to accomplish this goal. In longitudinal research we can begin to observe children and families in different contexts, and we observe them assuming different roles and positions within in those contexts. Instead of viewing a child at a particular time and place, we can see the same child fulfilling institutionally acceptable roles in one context and problematic roles in another; we see children flirting with positive student identities or claiming dominance on the playground. Rather than children fulfilling static roles as they move through school we see possibilities and opportunities for all children as they explore various ways of being. As educators we must recognize the multiple positionings that children assume and provide opportunities for children to create and develop new roles.

THE POSSIBILITY OF CHANGE

This book explores the literate lives of former students and their families whose words are not often heard by politicians, policy makers, or educators. Their silenced voices challenge each of us to think in new ways and consider new possibilities while questioning practices that we have not questioned in the past. How can we help children with their reading beyond telling them to sound out words? How can we help children to develop identities related to reading that lead to opportunities within school and beyond? How can we challenge the dominance of testing discourses that promise so much but offer so little to poor families of color? What do the stories of Marvin, Jermaine, Alicia, Jasmine, Peter, and Bradford tell us about creating classroom experiences that recognize their interests and developing identities? And finally, how can we recognize the strengths of all children while challenging official definitions of school and reading success?

Although these changes will take time and Herculean efforts from many people, I believe that change is ultimately inevitable and that educators can play an active and important role in supporting those changes. Alternative discourses reflect people's lived experiences. They challenge dominant discourses by challenging accepted ways of understanding the world. The very existence of these alternative discourses is the best evidence that change is possible. Alternative voices will always press upon dominant ways of understanding the world.

Consistent with the historically and socially constructed figured worlds of Holland et al. (1998), Norman Fairclough (1989) argues that the everyday worlds that people inhabit are riddled with assumptions and expectations that are "implicit, backgrounded, taken for granted" (p. 77). He argues that these ways of understanding the world are passed down over time through social institutions, including schools, and that accepted ways of understanding the world are deeply ingrained in our collective knowledge and generally remain unexamined.

This general acceptance of unexamined ways of understanding the world creates the possibility that people simultaneously ascribe to contradictory ways of understanding their worlds. As Fairclough (1995) describes, "It is quite possible for a social subject to occupy institutional subject positions which are ideologically incompatible, or to occupy a subject position incompatible with his or her overt political or social beliefs and affiliations, without being aware of the contradiction" (p. 42). Gunter Kress and Robert Hodge (1979) explain that this ability to hold contradictory views about the world is possible because the competing ideologies that accompany various views of the world are presented indirectly and implicitly and "act unconsciously, at a level beneath critical awareness" (p. 81). This unconscious nature allows all of us to unproblematically accommodate inconsistent and contradictory understandings of our worlds. However, the existence of contradictory ways of seeing the world does not silence critique; in fact Fairclough (1995) argues that the existence of the contradictions is not only the basis for awareness and reflexivity, but can also lead to change and agency.

I propose two practices—*third space* and *critical discourse analysis*—that I believe offer possibilities for my former students, their teachers, and their families. The existence of alternative discourses, such as those outlined in the first part of the book, and the contextualized issues explored in the second part of the book suggest that the constructs of third space and critical discourse analysis offer possibilities that will not only enable more students to succeed in schools but also provide parents and children with ways of talking back to dominant ways of speaking, thinking, and being.

Third Space

A range of theorists and researchers have contributed to current third space theories (Bhabha, 1994; Luke & Luke, 1999; Moje et al., 2004; Soja, 1996). I present conceptualizations of third space that offer possibilities for students. Moje and her colleagues (2004) describe a "'third space' that *merges* the 'first space' of people's homes, community, and peer networks with the 'second space' of the discourses they encounter in more formalized institutions such as work, school or church" (p. 41). These third spaces are hybrid spaces in which home and school categories of knowledge work together to create new kinds of knowledge and new ways of understanding the practices of both home and school.

Luke and Luke (1999) explain that third space must acknowledge and respect the histories that people bring. Thus, third space can be conceptualized as a site, or perhaps a moment, of hybridity in which words and meanings are reworked, renamed, and re-created. This interaction enables new positions and positionings to emerge that involve traces of the histories and identities that participants bring while creating new meanings and new understandings. Perhaps a hybrid discourse about urban families would include the firsthand stories of families and community members that would challenge popular conceptions of urban residents. Hybrid discourses would allow critiques of urban parents to be adapted into a more nuanced account in which people's literate practices, literacy experiences, daily challenges, and available resources are recognized. Educators can actively participate in the construction of this hybrid discourse by listening to parents and children, becoming open to alternative interpretations, and publicly voicing these alternative readings.

The research described on these pages presents a range of possibilities for creating third spaces that acknowledge and respect the histories and experiences that children bring to classrooms. Peter exchanges *Goosebumps* books with his friends and Marvin reads with his friend in the cafeteria. How can these reading experiences outside of the classroom enhance school reading practices? How might teachers build upon Jermaine's interest in looking at the pictures in nonfiction texts? What about the teen magazines that Jasmine enjoys, and Alicia's enthusiasm for being on the step team? Several of the children described their interest in hands-on science experiments and going on field trips. How can teachers show respect for them while using these experiences to create hybrid spaces in which home, peer, and school knowledges merge, extending each other while incorporating rich literacy practices?

Jasmine's case offers possibilities. Jasmine's teacher lets her select her own books to read. She writes about herself and is encouraged to incorporate popular media genres, a choose-your-own adventure story, which she casts with her friends and uses to examine the personally salient theme of friendship. However, across the study, descriptions of these types of experiences are not common. Most students describe their classrooms in terms of compliance, sometimes to teachers whom they depict as uncaring.

Yet third spaces cannot be limited to issues that occur within class-room walls. Third spaces between schools and classrooms, teachers and children, must incorporate the insights and interests of parents and families. Children do not leave their understandings and experiences behind when they come to school. They bring figured worlds and discourses that are historically situated in families and communities. Thus within classrooms dominant discourses pervade, and teachers are often complicent in the voicing of these generally unquestioned ways of being, acting, knowing, and believing. As teachers, we must constantly be aware that these dominant ways of understanding the world are not equally true for everyone. When teachers decry the communities that surround their schools, they must be aware that their students can tell alternative stories about their neighbors. When students get frustrated and angry with testing routines and may rightly suspect that their parents will never see their scores, they are often reluctant to buy into the testing mantras that promote doing their best on tests. Teachers must be ready to hear students voice both dominant and alternative discourses about their worlds and be willing to help students maneuver these tensions. Third spaces can be places where tensions can be named and examined. A significant aspect of being aware of the discourses that children bring means attending to the language they speak. Critical discourse analysis is a means to interrogate the words we use and the words our students use to better understand the ways we are all situated within institutionalized contexts that reward dominant ways of being and knowing.

Critical Discourse Analysis

Norman Fairclough reminds us that "language conventions and language practices are invested with power relations and ideological processes which people are often unaware of" (1993, p. 7). He espouses critical discourse analysis as a means to understand how texts, oral or written, function within sociocultural practices. He explains:

> Such analysis requires attention to textural form, structure and organization at all levels; phonological, grammatical, lexical (vocabulary) and higher levels of textual organization in terms of exchange systems (the distribution of speaking turns), structure or argumentation, and generic (activity type) structures. (1995, p. 7)

This type of analysis reveals how words position people, define issues, and construct particular versions of reality. Fairclough explains that power operates through various discourses that privilege the judgments made by particular groups of people.

Critical discourse analysis can fulfill three roles in schools and classrooms. First, teachers can use versions of critical discourse analysis to reveal how they and their students are positioned relative to curriculum mandates, state and national educational initiatives, and official school and district policies. Students can analyze "practice tests" to understand how tests act upon them and how right answers are the answers that makes sense to test makers. Textbooks can be analyzed for biases in terms of their presentation of various groups of people and the interpretations they bring to historical events: Which events are highlighted and which events are omitted?

Second, critical discourse analysis can be used to reflect on our own experiences and to reveal inequities in the educational systems in which we operate by revealing how teachers are positioned relative to parents and community members: What types of responses do parents receive when they voice their concerns at school? How are parents viewed by school communities? What is said in the staff lounge and how do these words position teachers and parents? This awareness on the part of teachers can lead to the creation of forums in which teachers listen to parents about their experiences. Alternative discourses can be voiced and expressed, and teachers can assume the role of learners rather than experts.

Finally, critical discourse analysis can be used by teachers to interrogate the words they use and the meanings those words bring to students. Peter Johnston has written an insightful book, *Choice Words* (2004), in which he challenges teachers to examine the language they use with children. When we tell children that they read well today, do we mean that the children got all of the words correct? Do we mean that they demonstrated a correct understanding of the story? Do we imply that they read poorly the day before, or do we mean that they behaved well in reading class?

In this book, I have used critical discourse analysis to explore conversations with parents and the ways children describe personal and school reading experiences. In some places, I attend to the ways parents and my former students express their ideas. Computers are described as "awesome," "right now," "the thing now-a-days"; they are everywhere and "everything." At other times, I highlighted participants' use of particular words and the ways those words position them and their neighbors; although parents speak disparagingly about urban parents in general, the words "my neighbor that lives downstairs" or "my next-door neighbor" mark very different understandings. At other times, I reflect upon the confidence or the hesitancy with which they express their ideas; comments about races are situated alongside markers of uncertainty: "I don't think so" or "not in my knowledge." Critical discourse analysis has helped me to better understand the situations and the lived realities of the children I teach and their families. I suspect that it can be equally illuminating for other classroom teachers.

RECOMMENDATIONS AND POSSIBILITIES

I suggest that we must remain aware of the many aspects of reading that go beyond decoding and fluency with text. We must create classrooms that draw children into social reading situations and actively challenge official notions of reading success. This research presents reading as one of many complex, situated abilities that can align and conflict with students' developing identities and are caught up in systems that constantly judge students and position them as successful or unsuccessful readers. This analysis suggests that educators should do the following:

- Consider students' interests and purposes for reading so that the strengths and knowledges they bring can be recognized and developed; Jasmine was allowed to use her own experiences to write adventure books that featured the girls in her classroom and their dramatic relationships with each other. Bradford was excited about lessons on Black history.
- Establish spaces where "unsuccessful" students can demonstrate their abilities and pursue their interests; integrate these strengths into literacy opportunities and classroom practices. While some students found spaces like the school cafeteria to utilize their reading abilities, these spaces and activities were not taken up by school personnel.
- Resist the tendency to define children as successful or unsuccessful; be on the alert for information and observations that contradict easy analyses about children; be ready to be surprised. Despite struggling to decode words, Bradford clearly understood what he read. While this ability defies logic, it is clearly a strength that teachers can capitalize upon. Reading is not a singular and finite skill and there are many ways of being an effective reader.
- Provide children with various experiences with reading and with their world: Incorporating various text/media genres, field trips, social opportunities, and hands-on experiences will enable more children to demonstrate their abilities. Several of the children in this study spoke extensively about the places they had visited with their classes and the importance these trips played in their lives.
- Foster rich relationships with parents so that their insights can inform our understandings of students and their abilities. Parents can often provide teachers with valuable information about interests, abilities, and experiences that young children do not reveal. With older children, parents often bring a different perspective to the stories that their children tell. Together the stories of parents and children offer complex and nuanced accounts that are extremely valuable to educators.
- Strive to learn about children's unexpected interests and abilities. The children in this study constantly surprise me. Every time I return to interview them I learn new information about the children and the richness of their lives. For example, in the 4 years since I was the children's teacher, I have learned that my former students sing in their church choirs, surf the Web, go on trips with local groups, and visit extended family members during summers.

Recognizing the range of experiences that children bring to classrooms challenges us to think carefully about what is defined as successful reading. Being responsive to that understanding involves changing, modifying, and expanding what we value in reading while recognizing that official reading success is often contingent on things that are only tangentially related to reading—sitting still, paying attention, sounding out words. Finally, we must recognize that some of things that we value in successful readers may not be displayed by all children and for good reasons. There are reasons why some children do not talk about school-approved texts in positive ways or do not take seriously testing programs that we assume will assess them as readers. There are reasons why they do not complete homework or write the kinds of stories that schools value. Sometimes children's experiences challenge the validity of our ways of being; too often the texts that teachers value in school do not speak of students' lives.

Current reading instructional programs tend to teach reading as if it were dissociated from other aspects of children's lives, and thus many children learn that school reading is not important. Despite this distancing, I remain encouraged and inspired by the many examples I have found of urban families who have found personal and collective reasons for reading and enjoy reading despite the negative experiences they may have experienced in school.

It seems clear to me from the 18 years I have spent teaching in urban and suburban schools that if we can ever begin to address the educational inequities of our society the answer will not lie in pedagogies, methods, or materials, but rather in attitudes and opportunities. The current educational system that we have established is little more than a mechanism for sorting children in relation to official school norms about literacy and life that ultimately value conformity and compliance.

The existence of alternative discourses provides hope. Ladson-Billings (2000) agrees: "Different discourses and epistemologies serve as both counter knowledge and liberating tools for people who have suffered (and continue to suffer) from the Euro-American 'regime of truth'" (p. 257). The mere existence of other ways of viewing the world continuously acts upon dominant discourses.

In this book, I have explored how the ways we think about reading and urban communities are situated within our own figured worlds that deny alternative ways of knowing. I use the stories of my former students and their families to present alternative possibilities. But dangers exist as well. Guadalupe Valdes (1996) writes of the struggle of Mexican Americans, explaining that "we can either advocate that Mexican communities and individuals be helped to make whatever changes are necessary to achieve success, or we can argue that there is already success among the population in question and that it is the majority society that must change its perspective" (p. 205). Is it the child who must acquiesce to the mainstream's ways of being and knowing, or do schools and the larger society have to change?

This path will be neither easy nor safe. We must remember that the indoctrination of particular forms of literacy is particularly insidious and often invisible to teachers and learners. My hope is that by finding ways to hear the stories of others and recognize them as situated within larger contexts, we can rise above this bifurcation of advocacy and celebration. We can recognize how we are all acted upon by discourses that confine and contradict, and it is through listening to alternative voices that we can begin to struggle through the tensions and challenge dominance.

Family Overviews

Parent/ Child	Age	Employment	Education	Family	Ethnicity
Ms. Burns	32	Grocery	Associate's	Married	European American
Angela	9	store	degree		European American
Ms. Hernandez	27	Dry	Not a	Single	Puerto Rican
Jasmine	9	cleaner	graduate		Puerto Rican
Ms. Holt	47	Disability	High school	Single	African American
Bradford	9		graduate		African American
Ms. Horner	29	Phone	GED	Married	African American
Peter	9	company			African American
Ms. Hudson	45	Disablilty	Not a	Married	African American
Jermaine	9		graduate, home/health certificate		African American
Ms. Johnson	38	Food	GED,	Widowed	European American
David	9	service	business school classes		Biracial
Ms. Mason	40	Pre-	High school	Single	African American
Javon	9	school	graduate		African American
Ms. Rodriguez	37	Day	GED,	Single	African American
Alicia	9	care	child care certificate		African American
Ms. Ross*	61	Day care	Not a graduate	Married	African American
Ms. Green-Abdul**	44	Disability	Associate's degree	Married	European American
Christy	10				Biracial
Mr. Sherwood***	52	Maintenance	High school graduate,	Married	African American
Marvin	10		trade school		African American

Parent/ Child	Age	Employment	Education	Family	Ethnicity
Ms. Webster§	32	Secretary	High school graduate, computer/ job training classes	Single	European American
Tiffany	9				Biracial

*Ms. Ross is Christy's foster mother; she had legal guardianship of Christy.

** Ms. Green-Abdul is Christy's biological mother.

***Mr. Sherwood is actually Marvin's stepgrandfather; he and Marvin's grandmother have primary responsibility for Marvin.

§ Ms. Webster participated in an earlier phase of the study.

Appendix B

Research Methodology

For my initial study, published as *Reading Families* (Compton-Lilly, 2003), I randomly chose 10 of my first-grade students and their parents to participate in a series of interviews focusing on concepts about reading; all names of people and places presented in both books are pseudonyms. The original study was conducted in a Northeastern midsized city that has the 11th highest rate of child poverty in the country. Rosa Parks Elementary School was a large urban school with a 97% poverty rate. At the time of the study, it was a "School in Performance Review" with the State Education Department due to several years of low test scores in reading. If scores failed to improve during the year of the initial study, the State Education Department had threatened to disband the school. During that year, I interviewed the children and parents about their experiences with reading and their lives.

At the time of the second phase of the study, three of the nine students interviewed this time still attended Rosa Parks Elementary School. Most of the children still lived within a 2-mile radius of their former school and attended other schools in the same district. The school where I was teaching during the second phase of the project, Henry Ford Elementary, was located one block away from the school in which the initial research was conducted. Henry Ford was a magnet school that attracted children from across the district and had a population of children that was similar to those at Rosa Parks School.

In order to understand how urban families' concepts about reading develop as children progress through school, I contacted 9 out of the 10 original families 3 years after the initial study. In this second phase of the study, I returned to interview my former students and their parents. One new family from my first-grade class was added to the research project to replace a child who could not be located during the second phase of the study. I purposely selected a fourth-grade student who had a younger sister in first-grade, the participating student grade that my former first graders should have been in during this second phase of the research. Two interviews were held during the school year when some of my former students were in fifth grade; others had been retained and were in fourth grade. Although prewritten questions directed at either my students, their parents, or their siblings were used at each interview, I encouraged subjects to elaborate on their comments, share related information, introduce issues that they felt were relevant, and pursue tangentially related issues. Specifically, the interviews explored the following topics:

- How my students and their families experience school reading practices over time
- How cultural practices related to reading within particular communities affect the ways students relate to school reading practices
- How my former students were constructing their identities as readers and as students
- How district, school, and classroom reading initiatives along with other social factors related to living in an urban community act upon children and families as children progress through school and develop as readers

Field notes were kept to contextualize my visits to students and their parents. I audiotaped and transcribed interviews with parents and students, analyzed student writing samples, conducted reading assessments with my former students, and obtained their fourth-grade state English Language Arts test scores.

After audiotapes were transcribed, each family was initially treated as a separate case. Data from each family were coded separately and an index was created for the data collected from each family to assist me in locating topics within the data sets. Coded data was grouped into categories of data for each family. Case studies were outlined for each family and recurring themes within families were noted. Cases that shared strong similarities or intriguing differences were linked and became the basis for Chapters 3, 4, and 5. I then reanalyzed data across the case studies to identify common themes and issues; dominant and alternative discourses became apparent at this point in the process. Finally, findings from this phase were compared to the data collected from these same families 4 years earlier when my students first learned to read. Data collection and analysis is an ongoing process as I continue to follow these students through their years in high school.

References

Adler, D., & Natti, S. (1992). *Cam Jansen and the mystery of the haunted house*. New York: Puffin.

Bakhtin, M. M. (1994). In P. Morris (Ed.), *The Bakhtin reader: Selected writings of Bakhtin, Medvedev, Voloshinov* (pp. 1–24). London: Edward Arnold.

Bartlett, L. (2005). Identity work and cultural artifacts in literacy learning and use: A sociocultural analysis. *Language and Education, 19*(1), 1–9.

Bartoli, J. S. (1995). *Unequal opportunity: Learning to read in the U.S.A.* New York: Teachers College Press.

Baskwell, J. (2006). If at first you don't succeed. . .: A closer look at an old adage. *Language Arts, 83*(6), 506–513.

Baumann, J.F., & Thomas, D. (1997). If you can pass Momma's tests, then she knows you're getting your education: A case study of support for literacy learning within an African American family. *The Reading Teacher, 51,* 108–120.

Beaver, J. (1997). *Developmental reading assessment*. Upper Saddle River, NJ: Pearson Learning Group.

Bhabha, H. (1994). *The location of culture*. London: Routledge.

Blues clues series. (1996–present). New York: Simon and Schuster.

Blume, J. (1972). *Tales of a fourth grade nothing*. Illustrated by R. Doty. New York: Dell.

Bourdieu, P. (1986). The forms of capital. In J. G. Richardson (Ed.), *Handbook of theory and research for the sociology of education* (pp. 241–258). New York: Greenwood Press.

Bridwell, N. (1963–present). *Clifford* series. New York: Scholastic.

Brown, M. (1976–present). *Arthur* series. New York: Little, Brown Young Readers.

Cappello, M. (2006). Under construction: Voice and identity development in writing workshop. *Language Arts, 83*(6), 482–491.

Clay, M. M. (1998). *By different paths to common outcomes*. York, ME: Stenhouse.

Clay, M. M. (2001). *Change over time in children's literacy development*. Portsmouth, NH: Heinemann.

Cleary, B. (1965). *The mouse and the motorcycle*. New York: HarperCollins.

Compton-Lilly, C. (2003). *Reading families: The literate lives of urban children*. New York: Teachers College Press.

Council of the Great City Schools. (2004, March). *Beating the odds IV: A city-by-city analysis of student performance and achievement gaps on state assessments: Results*

from the 2002–2003 school year. Retrieved April 27, 2006, from www.cgcs.
org/

Craighead, J. (1995). *There's an owl in the shower.* New York: HarperCollins.

Cummins, J, (1994). From coercive to collaborative relations of power in the
teaching of literacy. In M. Ferdman, R. Weber, & A. Ramirez (Eds.), *Literacy
across language and cultures* (pp. 259–331). Albany: State University of New
York Press.

Dahl, R. (1961). *James and the giant peach.* New York: Puffin.

Dahl, R. (1998). *Charlie and the chocolate factory.* New York: Puffin.

Davison, J., & Ford, D. (2002). Perceptions of attention deficit hyperactivity
disorder in one African American community. *Journal of Negro Education,
70*(4), 264–274.

De Castell, S., & Jenson, J. (2004). Paying attention to attention: New economies
for learning. *Educational Theory, 54*(4), 381–397.

Devine, J. (1994). Literacy and social power. In B. M. Ferdman, R. M. Weber, & A.
G. Ramirez (Eds.), *Literacy across languages and cultures.* Albany: State University
ty of New York Press.

Encisco, P. (2003). Reading discrimination. In S. Greene & D. Abt-Perkins (Eds.),
Making race visible: Literacy research for cultural understanding (pp. 149–177).
New York: Teachers College Press.

Fairclough, N. (1989). *Language and power.* London: Longman.

Fairclough, N. (1993). *Critical language awareness.* London: Longman.

Fairclough, N. (1995). *Critical discourse analysis: The critical study of language.* London:
don: Longman.

Ferdman, B. (1990). Literacy and cultural identity. *Harvard Educational Review,
60*(2), 181–204.

Fine, M. (1993). [Ap]parent involvement: Power, politics, and parents in urban
schools. *Teachers College Record, 94*(4), 682–710.

Fine, M. (2003). Silencing and nurturing voice in an improbable context: Urban
adolescents in public school. In M. Fine & L. Weis, (Eds.), *Silenced voices and
extraordinary conversations: Reimagining schools.* New York: Teachers College
Press.

Fine, M., & Weis, L. (1998). *The unknown city: The lives of poor and working-class
young adults.* Boston: Beacon Press.

Flores-Gonzalez, N. (2002). *School kids/street kids: Identity development in Latino
students.* New York: Teachers College Press.

Freebody, P., Forrest, T., & Gunn, S. (2001). Accounting and silencing in interviews: Smooth running through the "problem of schooling the disadvantaged." In P. Freebody, S. Muspratt, & B. Dwyer (Eds.), *Difference, silence and
textual practice: Studies in critical literacy* (pp. 119–152). Cresskill, NJ: Hampton
Press.

Freebody, P., Muspratt, S., & Dwyer, B. (2001). Preface. In P. Freebody, S. Muspratt, & B. Dwyer (Eds.), *Difference, silence and textual practice: Studies in critical
literacy* (pp. vii–xiv). Cresskill, NJ: Hampton Press.

Freire, P. (1986). *Pedagogy of the oppressed.* New York: Continuum.

Gallego, M., & Hollingsworth, S. (2000). Introduction: The idea of multiple literacies. In M. Gallego & S. Hollingsworth (Eds.), *What counts as literacy? Challenging the school standard.* New York: Teachers College Press.

Gee, J. P. (1990). *Social linguistics and literacies: Ideology in discourses.* London: Falmer.

Gee, J. P. (1992). *The social mind: Language, ideology and social practice.* New York: Bergin & Garvey.

Gee, J. P. (1996). *Social linguistics and literacies: Ideology in discourses* (2nd ed.). London: Taylor & Francis.

Gee, J. (1999). *An introduction to discourse analysis: Theory and method.* New York: Routledge.

Gee, J. P. (2000/2001). Identity as an analytic lens for research in education. *Review of Research in Education, 25,* 99–125.

Geertz, C. (1973). *The interpretation of cultures.* New York: Basic Books.

Gilbert, P. (1994). "And they lived happily ever after": Cultural storylines and the construction of gender. In A. H. Dyson & C. Genishi (Eds.), *The need for story: Cultural diversity in classroom and community.* Urbana, IL: National Council of Teachers of English.

Gilligan, C. (1982). *In a different voice: Psychological theory and women's development.* Cambridge, MA: Harvard University Press.

Godley, A. (2003). Literacy learning as gendered identity work. *Communication Education, 52*(3/4), 273–285.

Goines, D. (2000). *Eldorado red.* New York: Holloway House. (Original work published 1974)

Goines, D., & Locke, R. F. (1999). *Black girl lost.* New York: Holloway House.

Hare, H., & Orman, D. (2004, July 25). More and more getting degrees. *Rochester Democrat and Chronicle,* p. 10A.

Hawkins, M. (2005). Becoming a student: Identity work and academic literacies in early schooling. *TESOL Quarterly, 39*(1), 59–80.

Henkes, K. (1987). *Two under par.* New York: Puffin.

Hicks, D. (2002). *Reading lives: Working-class children and literacy learning.* New York: Teachers College Press.

Hillocks, G. (2002). *The testing trap: How state writing assessments control learning.* New York: Teachers College Press.

Holland, D., Lachicotte, W., Skinner, D., & Cain, C. (1998). *Identity and agency in cultural worlds.* Cambridge, MA: Harvard University Press.

Jacques, B. (1998). *Mossflower.* New York: Hutchinson Children's Books.

Johnston, P. H. (2004). *Choice words: How our language affects children's learning.* York, ME: Stenhouse.

Kress, G., & Hodge, R. (1979). *Language as ideology.* London: Routledge and Kegan Paul.

Ladson-Billings, G. (2000). Racialized discourses and ethnic epistemologies. In N. Denzin & Y. Lincoln (Eds.), *Handbook of qualitative research* (pp. 257–278). Newbury Park, CA: Sage.

Lanham, R. (1994). The economies of attention. *Proceedings of the Association of Research Libraries, 124.* Retrieved March 13, 2006, from http://sunsite. Berkeley.edu/ARL/Proceedings/124/ps2econ.html

Lewis, C. (2001). *Literary practices as social acts: Power, status, and cultural norms in the classroom*. Mahwah, NJ: Erlbaum.

Lewis, C. S. (1994). *The lion, the witch and the wardrobe*. New York: HarperCollins. (Original work published 1950)

Luke, A. (1996). Genres of power? Literacy education and the production of capital. In R. Hasan & G. Williams (Eds.), *Literacy in society* (pp. 308–338). New York: Longman.

Luke, A., & Luke, C. (1999). Theorizing interracial families and hybrid identity: An Australian perspective. *Educational Theory, 49*(2), 223–249.

Mahiri, J. (2001). Street scripts: African American youth writing about crime and violence. In P. Shannon (Ed.), *Becoming political, too: New reading and writings on the politics of literacy education* (pp. 67–87). Portsmouth, NH.: Heinemann.

Manhattan Institute for Policy Research. (2001). Civic report. Retrieved July 24, 2006, from http://www.manhattan-institute.org/html/cr_24.htm

Martin, A. M., & Lerangis, P. (1986–2000). *The babysitters club* series. New York: Scholastic.

McCarthey, S., & Moje, E. (2002). Identity matters. *Reading Research Quarterly, 37*(2), 228–238.

Michaels, B. (2000–2004). *Pokemon junior* series. New York: Scholastic Books.

Mishler, E. (1999). *Storylines: Craft artists' narratives of identity*. Cambridge, MA: Harvard University Press.

Moje, E., Ciechanowski, K., Kramer, K., Ellis, R., Carrillo, R. & Callazo, T. (2004). Working toward third space in content area literacy: An examination of everyday funds of knowledge and discourse. *Reading Research Quarterly, 39*(1), 38–70.

National Reading Panel. (2000). *Report of the National Reading Panel: Teaching children to read: An evidence-based assessment of scientific research literature on reading and its implications for reading instruction*. Washington, DC: National Institute of Child Health and Human Development, National Institutes of Health.

Nieto, S. (1996). *Affirming diversity: The sociopolitical context of multicultural education*. White Plains, NY: Longman.

Nuthall, G. (2005). The cultural myths and realities of classroom teaching and learning: A personal journey. *Teachers College Record, 107*(5), 895–934.

Park, B. (1993–present). *Junie B. Jones* series. New York: Random House.

Phillips, M., Brooks-Gunn, J., Duncan, G., Klebanov, P., & Crane, J. (1998). Family background, parenting practices, and the Black-White test score gap. In C. Jencks & M. Phillips (Eds.), *The Black-White test score gap* (pp. 103–148). Washington, DC: Brookings Institution Press.

Rayam, S., & Memmott, J. (2004, July 25). Recovering, rising. *Rochester Democrat and Chronicle*, p. 1A & 11A.

Rymes, B. (2001). *Conversational borderlands: Language and identity in an alternative, urban high school*. New York: Teachers College Press.

Sarup, M. (1996). *Identity, culture, and the postmodern world* (T. Raja, Ed.). Athens: University of Georgia Press.

Shanker, J., & Ekwall, E. (1999). Ekwall/Shanker reading inventory (4th ed.).

Needham Heights, MA: Allyn & Bacon.

Shannon, P. (2000). *iShop, you shop: Raising questions about reading commodities.* Portsmouth, NH: Heinemann.

Sharmat, M. W. (1972–2003). *Nate the Great* series. New York: Coward-McCann.

Smith, F. (2003). The just so story—Obvious but false. *Language Arts, 80*(4), 256–258.

Soja, E. W. (1996). *Third space: Journeys to Los Angeles and other real and imagined places.* Malden, MA: Blackwell.

Stine, R. L. (1989–present). *Fear street* series. New York: Parachute Press.

Stine, R. L. (1992–1997). *Goosebumps* series. New York: Scholastic.

Taylor, D., & Dorsey-Gaines, C. (1988). *Growing up literate: Learning from inner-city families.* Portsmouth, NH: Heinemann.

U.S. Department of Education. (2003a) *Guidance for the William F. Good-ling Even Start Family Literacy Programs: Part B, Subpart of Title I of the Elementary and Secondary Education Act (ESEA).* Washington, DC: Author.

U.S. Department of Education. (2003b). *No Child Left Behind: Choices for parents.* Retrieved August 21, 2006, from http://www.ed.gov/nclb/choice/index.html?src=ov

U.S. Department of Education. (2003c). *No Child Left Behind: Proven methods.* Retrieved August 21, 2006, from http://www.ed.gov/nclb/methods/index.html?src=ov

U.S. Department of Education. (2003d). *No Child Left Behind: Stronger accountability.* Retrieved August 21, 2006, from http://www.ed.gov/nclb/accountability/index.html?src=ov

Valdes, G. (1996). *Con respecto: Bridging the distances between culturally diverse families and schools: An ethnographic portrait.* New York: Teachers College Press.

Villenas, S., & Deyhle, D. (1999). Critical race theory and ethnographies challenging the stereotypes: Latino families, schooling, resilience, and resistance. *Curriculum Inquiry, 29*(2), 413–445.

Vygotsky, L. (1978). *Mind in society* (M. Cole, Ed.). Cambridge, MA: Harvard University Press.

Walkerdine, V. (1990). *Schoolgirl fictions.* New York: Verso.

White, E. B. (1952). *Charlotte's web.* New York: HarperCollins.

Wilson, W. (1998). The role of the environment in the black-white test score gap. In C. Jencks & M. Phillips (Eds.), *The black-white test score gap.* Washington, DC: Brookings Institute.

Zentella, A. C. (1997). *Growing up bilingual: Puerto Rican children in New York.* Malden, MA: Blackwell.

Index

About the Author

Catherine Compton-Lilly is Assistant Professor in Curriculum and Instruction at the University of Wisconsin at Madison. She taught in the public schools of New York State for 18 years. Catherine Compton-Lilly received her Ed.D. in Curriculum and Human Development from the University of Rochester in 1999. She is the author of *Reading Families: The Literate Lives of Urban Children* (Teachers College Press, 2003) and *Confronting Racism, Poverty and Power* (Heinemann, 2004). Dr. Compton-Lilly is the author of several articles and book reviews and is the editor-in-chief of *Networks*, a teacher research on-line journal. Recently, she was awarded a Spencer Small Grant that will enable her to complete the final phase of the research project described in this book now that her former students are in grades 10 and 11.